Appalachian Magazine's
Mountain Voice: 2017

*A Collection of Memories, Histories,
and Tall Tales of Appalachia*

DEDICATION

This publication is lovingly dedicated to the men and women of Appalachia. May the legacy of our ancestors shine for a thousand years.

Appalachian Magazine's Mountain Voice: 2017 is dedicated to serving as a living monument to the incredible lives of the men and women who call Appalachia home.

CONTENTS

The Story of Appalachian Magazine

How we were started

In December 2013, West Virginia native Jeremy T.K. Farley launched a blog sharing the many stories he had heard his grandparents recount of life in the coal mining towns of Mingo County. Within three months of the site's original launch, more than 3,000 people had subscribed to receive updates from the online publication and within a matter of days, *Appalachian Magazine* was born.

Photo: Appalachian Magazine Founders Allison & Jeremy Farley

Initially, just a blog he and his wife updated on a weekly basis, *Appalachian Magazine* has grown into one of the region's premier culture, history and travel publications, showcasing the Appalachian region's rich heritage, as well as the many businesses committed to moving the economy forward.

Today, *Appalachian Magazine* has over 68,000 Facebook fans and roughly a half-million monthly readers.

Our Mission & Passion

Being a native of Appalachia (Appa-LATCH-uh), Jeremy has a passion for the mountains, its people and history. This passion is felt in every article published on the website or printed in the publication's annual print edition (Congratulations on purchasing the inaugural issue!).

MISSION STATEMENT:

"The purpose of Appalachian Magazine is to showcase the tourism opportunities, rich history and timeless lifestyle of the greater-Appalachian region, while at the same time, providing a platform for frank and honest dialogue regarding the areas where improvement is needed."

The number of writers featured in both the online and print publication is ever growing and as the publication moves into the next phase of its existence, we remain committed to fulfilling our mission.

Appalachian Magazine's _Mountain Voice 2017_

Launched entirely as an online publication, Appalachian Magazine now receives daily requests from individuals desiring printed copies of articles they found on our website – many of these individuals wish to share these stories with loved ones who may not have Internet access, while others simply desire to hold in their hands the article in print-form.

Recognizing this growing demand and consumed with a desire to record the history, culture and way of life of our region for posterity, _Appalachian Magazine's Mountain Voice 2017_ was conceived – a printed book containing a series of copyrighted anthologies of articles originally written online, along with additional content not suitable for the online format.

Appalachian Magazine is a labor of love and readers can expect for _Appalachian Magazine's Mountain Voice 2017_ to be merely the first of several dozens of years' worth of printed publications containing the previous year's top articles… That is, Lord willing… and the creeks don't rise!

Thank you for supporting our passion.

To invite Jeremy Farley to a speaking engagement, please contact via the email listed below:

We'd love to hear from you, keep in touch:

Facebook:
Facebook.com/AppalachianMagazine

Twitter:
@AppalachianMag

Email:
publisher@appalachianmagazine.com

Website:
www.AppalachianMagazine.com

Appalachian Magazine

Travel, History, Life.

My Mountain Memories

My Mother Making Me Catch the Measles

Written by George Houston in 1904

And here, [Eastern Kentucky] I was born in the year that my grandfather died. There were already three children in the family, but they were all daughters. My father and mother both ardently wished for a son and there was great rejoicing over the birth of the first boy when I appeared at last on the fifth of February 1821.

There was no physician in the neighborhood at that time. Doctors were indeed few and far between in my own recollection. But trusty midwives were to be had and the most widely and well known of these was Aunt Franky McFarland, a large fleshy old woman who rode a black horse.

She was summoned from far and near and came eight miles to assist in bringing me into the world.

My earliest distinct recollection goes back to a time when I could not have been over four years old.

In the fall of that year my father, who was always fond of hunting in a country abounding in game, took me out for a little hunt. He soon found a squirrel in the top of a tree.

Pointing to the small bunch of gray fur he shot and down came the squirrel.

I ran and picked it up, but the little creature was only wounded and grasped my left hand in his teeth and firmly held on to his bite. Pain and fright caused me to scream. Father freed my hand and after killing the squirrel carried me home in his arms.

To this day I bear scars showing the marks of the squirrel's teeth.

Another very early experience that impressed itself upon me was going with my elder sister to the house of a neighbor in order to get the measles, and this I believe occurred in the same year.

It is hard to understand the reason for taking such a step as this, possibly, may have been regarded at that time when medical science thereabouts was in its infancy, much as vaccination or inoculation is regarded in these days.

At all events, the heroic measure proves my mother to have been a woman of courage of firmness and great strength of character one who was able to do what was generally thought to be the best in the face of all her natural fears.

Accordingly, we were sent in the charge of Aunt Nancy and told to kiss the children who had the complaint which was then prevalent in the neighborhood.

We did as directed and both my sister and I forthwith took the disorder and certainly had it quite as thoroughly as could have been desired.

And during the entire time that we were ill with the measles we were confined to a dark room and allowed scarcely any food and were given nothing to drink but nauseous hot teas made out of the leaves of the sage bush or the bark of sassafras roots.

And even these drinks were without sweetening for mischief was then supposed to lurk in sugar.

Long years after my Aunt Nancy told me that the main purpose in sending us was to insure our having the disease in the spring of the year when it was thought to be less dangerous than at any other season.

If so, the purpose was served — for when we were permitted to look out of the window the apple trees were in bloom truly a beautiful and charming sight for children in our condition.

Memories of a West Virginia's Slave Market

Appalachian Magazine Staff

In the days leading up to the American Civil War, Wheeling, Virginia, grew into an important stop along the underground railroad, standing as it does between Ohio and Pennsylvania.

Many runaway slaves would enter into the city by darkness of night and find lodging courtesy of the A.M.E. Zion Church and the proprietor of the Wheeling House Hotel, who would arrange safe houses for runaways.

One local family, the McKeever's, would hide fugitive slaves in their poultry wagon and drive them to freedom in Pittsburgh.

Despite these gems of humanity, slavery existed in this Virginia region which stretched farther north than Staten Island.

At the epicenter of slavery in this peninsula of bondage was the Wheeling Market House, where weekly slave auctions were held

Located along the National Road and on the banks of the Ohio River, Wheeling, Virginia was ideally suited for slave trade, as purchased individuals would often be barged down the Ohio to places in the Deep South.

Thomas B. Seabright, in his history of the National Road, wrote: "Negro slaves were frequently seen on the National Road. They were driven over the road arranged in couples and fashioned to a long, thick rope, or cable, like horses."

Joseph Bell, born in 1819, remembered seeing on Wheeling streets, "gangs of slaves chained together, women as well as men, on their way south. As a little boy, I remember standing on the sidewalk with my brother when such a gang was passing. We were eating an ear of corn apiece, which some of the slaves begged from us."

According to historians, the ringing of the market bell would signify to the community of Wheeling that a slave trade was about to begin.

Judge John Cochran, wrote of his early visits to the slave auction as a young child:

"Saturday morning in June while attending this market at the age of ten years and while gratifying our idle curiosities as boys will sometimes do I with a neighbor boy sauntered to the upper end of the markethouse and there beheld a sight which I shall never forget and which afterwards changed my whole political thought and action. It was a slave auction.

The auction block was on the west side of the upper end of the market about where the city scales are now located. It was a wooden movable platform about two and a half feet high and six feet square approached by some three or four steps. The auctioneer was a little dapper fellow with a ringing voice and an air of self-important bustle which to a boy bespoke him a man of surprising importance. Not a very large crowd was surrounding the auction block. On top of it was a portly and rather aged negress and the auctioneer. She was a mulatto had a broad full face a soft matronly eye and gray hair. Her look was all kindness and affection though now it wore a sad and troubled expression, I liked her as soon as I saw her.

Grouped together on the ground at the side of the block stood three other negroes two men and one woman. They were all about the same age the woman, being probably two years younger than the men and aged about twenty. She was also a mulatto, as was one of the men, while the other who was her brother was quite dark with features and expression like his mother on the auction block. In outline of form and face the girl looked like her mother and darker brother though here as to the brother the resemblance ended. She was tall and slender with a queenly grace and voluptuous swell of chest and gave evidence of refinement not looked for in a slave. Her lips were thin as those of a white person and her eyes quite dark. They were full of tears.

I thought her lovely. She was almost white and her hair while wavy was not short and tight curled like her brother's, but long and jet black. Had she been in Spain, no question would have been made that she was a Spaniard.

In my childish innocence, I could not reason how this girl could be the sister of that black brother. Subsequent knowledge has taught me my mistake, though only half a mistake after all. It arose from the conditions of American slavery. What a contradiction of words American slavery. And yet it was true!

Then her head fell again and when I quietly slipped around in front of her and looked up into her face the tears were freely rolling over her cheeks down onto her blue checked apron. I knew something was wrong and I wanted to give relief. I pulled the coat tail of an elderly gentleman and when he stooped down to know what I wanted he answered my inquiry by saying this was a slave auction and they were going to sell these four colored people.

He told me they would likely be purchased by different buyers and be separated for life — that the woman on the block was the mother of the black man and mulatto girl and that the other mulatto man and they all belonged to one master who

Photo: Dated 15 April 1865, "Aunt Susan" a slave woman tending a white baby. Back of image contains 2 cent tax stamp and photographer's name, "Brown & Lose, Photographers, Wheeling, W.Va.

had broken up and they were being sold to pay creditors. This elderly gentleman seemed so kind. He had a light brown broad brimmed hat and was dressed in drab colored clothes with clean white shirt and close fitting standing collar. His coat came up and fastened close to the neck like that of a minister He seemed educated and refined. His clothes, I noticed, had some flour on them. When he began to talk to me I saw at once he was a Quaker and for the first time I looked at his face and knew him at once...

When I asked why they were selling these poor people he replied, 'For money, my child, the price of human blood.' His words were subdued and low, as though he wanted no one but me to hear, but I noticed the young mulatto girl caught every word he said and her face lighted up with a

16

strange hope.

'What will they do with them, Mr Cope, when they buy them?' I asked, 'Take them away to the South and work them like beasts just as we do horses and oxen without pay or reward,' he replied, 'Some of them are cruelly beaten and mistreated, though this is not often done by the masters, as it is not to their interest to do so. It is ordinarily done by their slave drivers without the knowledge of the owners. They are mere employees who work on a salary and try to make a big showing at the end of the year by increased crops at the physical expense of the slaves in order to retain their positions. One of the worst features of this accursed traffic is the separation of families husband and wife, parent and child, brother and sister. But this is not all my child,' here his voice dropped to almost a whisper, 'this is not the worst, would to God it were!'

'You do not know now, but you will when you are older Some masters are not content to own the bodies they are ruining the souls of their female slaves. Oh my boy, God is gathering a swift and terrible judgment to the people who are doing these things. If you live, you will see terrible times for these wrongs. Be a man when it comes.'

Southwest Virginia Saturday Nights

Written by Anna Wess

I remember you. And I remember much more than just your name. And you could say the same of me, if you'd choose. We share the same memories, you and I, of places and names and faces and feelings that we can recall with a few old lyrics or a local stranger's recollection. We both grew up here in this nowhere town, this speck of geography that only God knows well, a place too small for any nobody who is anybody to know of completely. Not like we do, at least.

It doesn't matter who else knows us. Not at all. We are big fish in a little pond. The best of ponds, and the best of fish. We know hardship and loss and tragedy. We have, together, shared them all. There wasn't a dry eye in town the day the sweet Harman girl was summoned away, to be forever seventeen. Or when Brad was lost to Heaven that night in the fog on the mountain, to be young and beautiful for eternity, as we know it. We all knew about them within the stretch of a few morning hours, if not less.

We know the same tragedies, of course. But few know the nights, the nights when we were young and full of guts and gumption, the nights we spent mingling our lives together while claiming Richlands and making it ours, when anybody who was anybody was there. And we were there, too. Once upon a sometime, we knew and loved each other just because we knew nothing else to do. We were bound together by commonplace and Garth Brooks songs and our aforementioned tragedies. We knew her. We knew him. We knew Garth. We danced beneath the stars together in fields we were forbidden to dance in and talked about our friends in low places and looked forward to the tomorrows that we knew, despite our years, would all too soon, be yesterdays.

And at this moment, yesterday is now, and our lost friends have been dead much longer than they ever lived, and yet we remember them still. Beyond them, we remember those of us that are still here to tell of those good times, when we were untouched by formal education and ponds bigger than ours, untainted by places other than Honaker and Grundy and our own dear Richlands. When Jewell Ridge was a trip all by itself, and we didn't worry about cell service; we didn't know a cell phone from the boogey man or electric bills or the cost of baby formula. We were our own babies then, though we would have never admitted it to each other.

And beyond ourselves, we picture the stories that our mamas told, of how that Combs boy went full crazy with youth and moxie and streaked, just like that Ray Stevens account, across Ernie Hicks field after graduation, and up into the woods behind the water tank, naked as a jaybird, and that only a stadium full of Richlands folk would have cheered and praised the Lord for forgiveness at the same blessed time. Oh, what a sight it must have been.

But those days are long passed, and so are the we that we remember. But some things are everlasting, and you and I are a few of those things. Unlike our long gone friends—the Harman girl, sweet Brad, Sam and Heather, and Shawn and Curtis, the Cole and Harrison boys and the other big fish in this little pond that have already been caught, God rest their young souls—we remain. Whether we are still at home or have ventured into the wild yonder, we are still here. And it has been half our lives since those Southwest Virginia Saturday nights. And yet we can close our eyes for only a moment, and recollect your innocent face, conjure up the remnants of an old song or two, and we are right back where it began. Where we began.

We wake up some nights even now, after our children have gone on to dream, and lament the vapors of our old selves that have drifted into some blue yonder, to only be known in spirit and memory. And we will miss each other. And it is there that I will know you, in that some azure somewhere. And love you, my friend, in that low place.

We are twice as old as we were then. If not a few years more.

Some things change. Some things don't. The same could be said for people. For us, too. But you know so much more than my name, and I could say the same for you. We are the best of big fish, in the best of little ponds.

And the best of the best ain't been caught yet.

This article was written by Anna Wess. Anna is an Appalachian native, raised in Southwest Virginia, a stone's throw from Kentucky, West Virginia, Tennessee, and North Carolina. She has been a writer for the better part of thirty years. She periodically posts various writings on her blog, Appalachian Ink.

Losing Our Appalachian Mountain
Appalachian Magazine Staff

Photo: Appalachian Mountains, courtesy of Brian Stansberry

Mary Whalen is a retired nurse/teacher who lives with her husband on a chicken farm in Northern Kentucky. Her article, "Predator-Proof Chicken Coop", has appeared in Backwoods Home Magazine, May/June 2016

In the fall of '96, when the crisp leaves of the oak and ash and walnut and hickory trees were turning red, orange, and brown, and the smell of bonfires spoke of the end of hot summer nights, my husband lost his job and we lost our church, in the same month.

Don't ask me to explain the church incident. It turned into a blessing and a healing though, because with our foundations cracked, we found ourselves suddenly able to gratify a long abandoned wanderlust. We left our home in Cincinnati, to explore the mountains of southeastern Kentucky.

We needed solace.

We enjoyed lunch at a small town, and on a local realtor's tip, we bounced along a one-lane overgrown trail forgotten by time and happened upon—a mountain.

We did a little research. It was a peak in the Appalachian basin, sometimes called the hill country, but anything I have to crane my head back and not see the top of, is a mountain to me. It rose above a stream with a pasture of gently rolling spurs drawn up to coniferous peaks. An old decrepit barn stood sentry near the stream.

We'd heard from the realtor that bear, red fox, deer and rattlesnake were the only inhabitants of this property. We found out differently.

After giving us uncertain directions, the realtor explained that it would be best if we were friendly to everyone we met as "you don't want to cross anyone, you know what I mean?" We weren't really sure what he'd meant.

The mountain was covered with logged over rutted roads that seemed too narrow for our Tracker to navigate. We also discovered from the deeps of the forested trails, that at three o'clock in the afternoon, it looked like the sun was about to set. At three o'clock in the afternoon!

My husband, John, is of Scots-Irish descent whose relatives originally came from Scotland to County Waterford, Ireland in the 17th century and thence by way of New York, to Kentucky He has inherited this spirit of adventure. He's a hard working man who doesn't know when to quit. I could see the wheels turning in his mind, thinking of all the things he would do with this property. Maybe start marking trees so we could widen one of the many roads on the mountain, or build a small cabin.

We headed back to town and bought the place.

The next day, we came back and headed up the widest road on the mountain, noting bear tracks in the dirt, when

Photo: *Where we got stuck, Submitted*

suddenly our little green Tracker sank into a ditch the size of Manhattan. Upon walking down to the flat area by the stream, we heard a car coming down another road on the other side of the mountain.

It was a small car driven by a very young couple. The young lady in the front passenger seat was holding an infant in her arms.

"What's the problem?" the fella asked. We explained our dilemma and directly, the girl handed me the infant and said they would be back with help. Here I was in the growing dusk, in a place I didn't know, holding a baby I didn't know. Maybe it wasn't true that mountain people were not friendly.

Not ten minutes later, we heard sound of machinery coming from other side of the creek. Sure enough, the couple brought help in the form of a tractor and a strong looking red headed driver.

Our car was freed from the ruts in minutes. My husband offered some of the fallen trees left over from logging, as a gesture of appreciation. Our young savior offered his hand and smiled. "Name's Smith," he said before roaring away in a blue cloud of tractor smoke.

The young girl matter-of-factly took the baby back from my arms, and away they went too.

Even as dusk was upon us, we figured that we still had time to travel past our mountain in an opposite direction from the road we came in on, when we noticed a older fellow heading our way through the tall grass by the barn. He was a wiry, spare man, wearing a slouched, tan hat.

We hollered "Hello!" No answer.

As he got nearer, John extended his hand, said hello again, and introduced himself, explaining why we were there. When John mentioned our realtor's name, the man, who acknowledged his name as Will, gave us a half smile, and shook John's hand.

Photo: John Marking Trees, Submitted

"I'm the only neighbor you'd have around here", he explained, eyeing us up and down. "I keep a lookout on all this property." I put on my friendliest smile.

We talked for awhile and he suggested that we drive on past his house down the road "a piece". "You'll see where I live. You'll also find a mighty old post office but it ain't used anymore", he said.

Our interest

piqued, we crossed the creek again and turned left and there was his cabin. It had a large front porch, and a scattering of chickens clucking their way around the front yard, and there on the porch were several rockers. On one sat a woman that must have been his wife, and on another sat an even older lady, a wizened matriarch it seemed, with iron gray hair in a bun.

There were several children of various sizes hanging around the porch, all grinning and waving to beat the band. If we'd been mountain folks already, we'd have gotten out and said hello. I reflected that city people need to be initiated in the art of neighborliness.

We waved back, while driving slowly down the graveled road.

The road became narrower as we went along. A mile or two later, the gravel became a desolate creek bed. There was nowhere else to turn, and no other road, so we continued on. The creek bed became a dead end. No post office in sight, in fact, no road left at all. If we hadn't had this small car that took us twenty minutes to turn around in, we would still be there. I wondered if even God knew where we were.

With the approach of deep evening shadows, we once again passed Will's house on the right, and we could see that they were on the porch, still rocking, still grinning, the kids still laughing, and the chickens still clucking. Well we laughed right back. We'd been had. I loved that our neighbors had a sense of humor. Being able to share a laugh over something with someone makes me feel welcome.

On subsequent visits, before actually investing in materials to build a small cabin, we explored and tramped around the mountain and also explored our growing friendship with our neighbors. We planted turnips in the field by the creek, at our new neighbor's suggestion, to attract the deer, both for our neighbors and ourselves' sustenance.

Over the next few weeks, we found our new adventures in the hills positively rapturous, —we also found we had an unexpected, exorbitant tax bill from the city we left behind that we had no money for. It seems that when you sell a house in a populated area in the big city, and plunk down a much smaller amount in a rural, mountainous area, the Federal government steps rights up to claim their due.

We had to sell the mountain property. It hurt.

We and our neighbor and his kindly wife, whom we officially met on our second foray into this wilderness, exchanged letters and greeting cards over the next few years.

After a while, we lost touch. We never went back.

We thought of it.

We had learned first-hand something of Appalachian culture, and people. We loved the warm embrace of mountain ridges that spoke of history and strife and of a type of strength and resiliency not known to city folks. I felt safe there. We had fallen in love with the people. Their pioneering spirit resonated with ours.

It's been twenty years, and it still stings when it comes to mind what we lost.

Eventually we found a farm in a spot nearer to northern Kentucky and raised a bunch of cattle, goats, sheep, and most numerous of all, chickens. We learned to live off the land, but never forgot our first dream of living in the mountains, and understanding a people that settled our country. It was the adventure we almost had.

Would it look the same to me if we went back someday? Maybe, but I think my heart would ache.

Since then, I have studied more about the Appalachian people; their unique struggles and heartwarming graciousness. I wish I was one of them.

The Real Reason My Grandfather's Family Had a "Dinner Bell"

Appalachian Magazine Staff

In the quiet coalfields of southern West Virginia there is a simple brick house. The house sits at the edge of a steep mountain and overlooks one of over a hundred streams and creeks in the area.

At the back of this house there is a pole and at the top of that pole there is a simple and unsuspecting red bell. Though faded and leaning sharply, the heavy piece of steel continues to watch over my great-grandfather's backyard, as it has my entire life, and for that matter, most of his.

Today, the bell is nothing more than just another overlooked lawn ornament dotting the West Virginia landscape. Nothing different from the dozens of flag poles, painted rocks and porcelain objects scattered across all the other yards of his aging community.

Once upon a time, however, this innocent looking bell was the only thing that stood between my relatives and revenuers intent upon cracking down on the region's prevalent moonshine industry.

According to my 91-year-old great-grandfather, a century ago, large bells like the one pictured were not only visible on his property, but on nearly all of the tracts of land adjoining the small stream known as Elk Creek – all part of a well-orchestrated, defense network designed to notify Mingo County's brewers of strangers being spotted in the area.

"I remember going with my dad to visit my aunt who lived just a ways up the hollow, when I was just a young boy," my great-grandfather whispered to me, in a frail and weak voice that seemed so foreign from the deep, proud and crackling tone I will always remember him having.

Pausing just long enough to catch his escaping breath, he continued, "Every time we'd get there, I would ask her where my older cousins were and she'd always say that they were up in the woods looking for some hogs that had gotten out."

"I always thought it was odd that their hogs would get out so often, and one day I finally said, 'You fellers need to build a better hogpen' and my dad and aunt both started laughing!"

"One day, while we were there, a black car drove by and she jumped to her feet and ran out the back of the house. Within a matter of seconds, every bell within a few miles was ringing and a couple of minutes afterward, here come my cousins running out of the mountains."

Today, the exploits of coldblooded killings taking place outside train tunnels and prevalence of illegal whiskey distilling is a piece of Bloody Mingo's history many of the residents would just assume forget; however, there is one West Virginia resident – nearly a century old – who will never forget the true reason there are so many of those peculiar looking "lunch bells" in the coalfields of the Mountain State.

Appalachian Histories
and Tales of the Past

Granny Women: Appalachia's Original Medical Professionals

Appalachian Magazine Staff

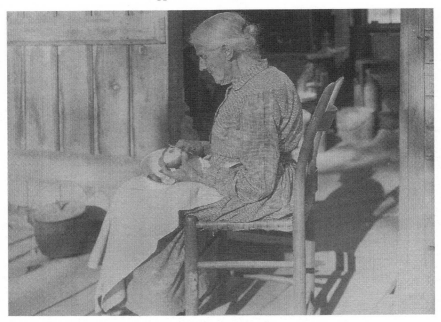

Not many days after first arriving in the New World, the fiercely independent Scots-Irish would

Separating themselves from other medical workers, Granny Women fancied themselves to not have expected or received payment for their services and were viewed as critical elements to mountain life.

In 1921, John C. Campbell wrote about the remaining Granny Women of Appalachia:

There is something magnificent in many of the older women with their stern theology—part mysticism, part fatalism—and their deep understanding of life. Patience, endurance, and resignation are written in the close-set mouth and in the wrinkles about the eyes; but the eyes themselves are kindly, full of interest, not unrelieved by a twinkling appreciation of pleasant things. 'Granny'

'Granny' —and one may be a grandmother young in the mountains—if she has survived the labor and tribulation of her younger days, has gained a freedom and a place of irresponsible authority in the home hardly rivaled by the men of the family. Her grown sons pay to her an attention which they do not always accord

their wives; and her husband, while he remains still undisputed master of the home, defers to her opinion to a degree unknown in her younger days. Her daughters and her grandchildren she frankly rules. Though superstitious she has a fund of common sense, and she is a shrewd judge of character. In sickness, she is the first to be consulted, for she is generally something of an herb doctor, and her advice is sought by the young people of half the countryside in all things from a love affair to putting a new web in the loom.

It is not surprising if she is something of a pessimist on the subject of marriage. 'Don't you never get married' is advice that is more than likely to pass her lips.

Many of these Granny Women's words of wisdom have been lost to time, but chances are that the majority of our readers are far more familiar with some of these women's words of wisdom than we may initially care to admit. Thanks to these women, we all grew with the understanding that the cure for an earache is urine!

Why the Old Timers Would Sweep Their Yards

Appalachian Magazine Staff

"Back when I was a kid, there wasn't a single blade of grass growing in our front yard. Between us kids playing all day and my mamaw sweeping the front yard on a daily basis, grass didn't stand a chance at growing," recalls one reader.

But why? Where did this classically southern tradition come from and why would women take the time to painstakingly sweep their yards each day in generations past?

A 1993 article that first appeared in the New York Times set out to answer this question, with writer Anne Raver stating, "Blacks here, descendants of slaves brought mainly from West Africa to work the cotton fields in Georgia's hard clay, are carrying on the traditions that their ancestors brought from the Gold Coast... And the swept yard was the most important 'room' of the household, the heart of the home. Slave quarters were cramped and hot. So you washed and cooked outside, and when the meal was over, everything could be swept into the fire."

According to the article, the custom quickly grew into mainstream throughout the South and soon, "Almost everybody had swept yards, including the plantations, which were swept by slaves or servants..."

Turns out, the idea of lawn sweeping grew out of practicality as much as anything. In an era long before Cub Cadet and John Deere, keeping one's lawn free of overgrown weeds was a tall order.

With heavy populations of venomous snakes ranging from the Appalachian Mountains to the South Carolina low country, the fear of having their homes (which weren't sealed off very well to begin with) invaded by an unwelcomed serpent led the nation's inhabitants to take some pretty drastic measures — sweeping their yard.

By sweeping their yards down to the dirt, early homesteaders were able to establish a perimeter around their homes which would ensure a safe play area for their children, as well as provide an indicator as to whether their dwelling places had been visited by a snake.

Often, it was the job of the children to go outside and circle around the house each morning, checking for snake tracks. If the tracks led to under the home, the entire family would put everything they were doing on hold until the snake was found.

This was common practice throughout most of America's history, in fact, it wasn't until the mid-1800s that many Americans started keeping lawns, and even then, it was done only by the very wealthy as a status symbol — a practice that was adopted from European royalty.

"At first, only the wealthy could afford the labor provided by hired staff to maintain lawns so of course, this further cemented the idea of lawn as a status symbol," writes The Garden Diva.

So if you can remember the sight of mamaw sweeping the front yard, count yourself fortunate, knowing that she was doing so out of a love for you and for your protection!

Feedsack Fashion

Appalachian Magazine Staff

Desperate times call for desperate measures and few times in our nation's long history have been as trying as the days of the 1930's during America's Great Depression.

With cotton at a premium and money scarce, the citizens of America's heartland and Appalachian Mountains found themselves with few options with regards to clothing their growing children in the days leading up to the Second World War.

Ultimately, relief came from a very unsuspecting place: the heavy feed and flour sacks that served as the staple product purchased by rural America.

Soon, mothers from rural-Virginia to the Great Plains were cutting the empty sacks into patterns, sewing them into dresses and pants for their needy sons and daughters. They weren't pretty, but the flour sacks served a much-needed purpose.

Though a great example of American ingenuity, the idea of turning flour sacks into clothes was not an American invention.

As early as 1904, Chinese peasants had been wearing trousers made from flour sacks, garnering the outfits the humble title of "hunger clothes."

Once American flour companies caught wind of the fact that their bags were being used to clothe children, they began printing the sacks with various patterns that would make for pretty dresses and soon, mother's were basing their flour purchases based upon the prints of the bag.

Kendra Brandes of Bradley University writes:

The recycling of cotton feed sacks into apparel and household items was a common practice across rural America during the first half of the twentieth century. This creative recycling of a utilitarian fabric has, until recently, been omitted from histories of American fashion because the practice centered on fabric use rather than new garment styles, and because the farm wife of rural America was not considered to be a source of fashion inspiration... However, it is the activities of these farm wives, clothing their families in feed sacks, that offer a view of life that was unique to rural communities during this time period.

Though born of necessity, the wearing of feed sacks proved to be one of the defining character builders of a generation that would ultimately defeat Hitler, land a man on the moon and overcome one of the worst economic depressions the world has ever known. Well done, mom!

Appalachian Language:
"Lord Willing and the Creek Don't Rise"
Appalachian Magazine Staff

My grandmother was a five-foot nothing tower of a mountain woman whose tenacious spirit was seconded only by her faith in the Divine and commitment to His holy book.

On far more than one occasion, I had the good pleasure of having my sentence extended by her, as she would add "If the Lord wills." Looking back, it's clear that granny knew something it has taken me decades to realize: the best made plans of mice and men often stay as just that – plans.

Her almost obsessive desire to add "if the Lord wills" to the end of anyone's plan came from the fourth chapter of the New Testament book of James:

"Whereas ye know not what shall be on the morrow. For what is your life? It is even a vapour, that appeareth for a little time, and then vanisheth away. For that ye ought to say, If the Lord will, we shall live, and do this, or that."
— James 4.14-15

Photo: *Destroyed railroad and highway bridge after the November 4-5, 1985, flood of the Cheat River in Rowlesburg, West Virginia*

Though you will be hard pressed to find anyone who was as faithful to this Christian commandment or took it as literal as she did, if you spend any length of time at all in Appalachia, you will probably hear someone state, "Lord willing and the creek don't rise."

Or is it "Lord willing and the Creeks don't rise"?

Now that's the true question!

There are multiple flood warnings and watches throughout nearly of Appalachia tonight and as I continue to monitor the creek just outside my window, I'm reminded of my grandmother and this timeless idiom.

According to one writer, the expression "Lord willing and the creek don't rise" is "an American slang expression implying strong intentions subject to complete frustration by uncommon but not unforeseeable events. It presumably evokes occasional and unpredictably extreme rainfall in Appalachia, that has historically isolated one rural neighborhood or another temporarily inaccessible on several or many occasions" and when most folks in the mountains use this term, that is exactly what they mean.

Classic versions of its use tend to be along the lines of "The good Lord willing, and creek doesn't rise"—i.e. "If God so wills, and as long as intense rain does not wash away bridges or parts of dirt roads, or cover roads too deeply for safely following them." It may take the form of real or mock dialect, in variations like "... Lor' willin' an' th' crick don' rise."

Interestingly, there are some linguists who have argued that the "C" in creek should actually be capitalized and that the original saying was intended to mean if the "Creek" Indian tribe didn't rise up.

Some historians attribute Benjamin Hawkins as having been the first person to ever say these words and he did so in a letter to the President of the United States.

Hawkins served under George Washington as General Superintendent for Indian Affairs (1796–1818) and had responsibility for the Native American tribes south of the Ohio River, and was principal Indian agent to the Creek Indians.

In a letter to the Commander in Chief, Hawkins stated that he would return to the nation's capital, "God willing and the Creek don't rise."

"Hawkins, college-educated and a well-written man would never have made a grammatical error, so the capitalization of Creek is the only way the phrase could make sense... and the reference is not to a creek, but The Creek Indian Nation. If the Creek 'rose', Hawkins would have to be present to quell the rebellion." writes one commentator.

However the belief that this universally used mountain saying is not in reference to rising water is not universally accepted by those who have studied the history of this phrase.

Another commentator was rather blunt in his assessment of the above theory:

"The idea, espoused below, that the remark should be attributed to Benjamin Hawkins is patently ridiculous. If you read the history attached to the citation, you'll see that Hawkins was devoted to the Creek. He married his common-law Creek wife on his death bed. The Creek were at peace during most of Hawkins' tenure as Superintendent of the Tribes of the Ohio River. Although there was an uprising by the Red Sticks, part of the Creek nation, Hawkins would not have referred to them generically as Creek because he was trying to protect the Creek nation from being penalized for the actions of the Red Sticks."

Regardless of what served as the inspiration to this timeless phrase, the reality is that it has caught on and in today's world, there is very little chance of a Creek uprising; however, as streams and rivers are rising across the region with these late-April showers, the creeks are bound to rise!

As most water deaths occur in vehicles, perhaps this old saying can take on new meaning — turn around, don't drown... and get there only if the good Lord's willing and the creek don't rise!

The Story Behind
"More ___ Than Carter's Got Liver Pills"
Appalachian Magazine Staff

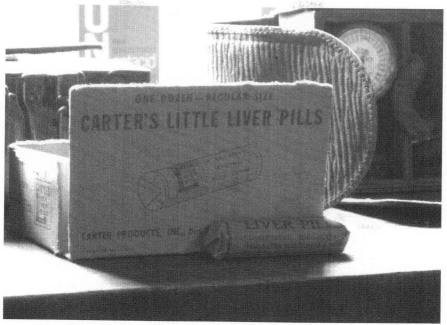

Photo: Carter's Little Liver Pills. Courtesy jennandjon

Growing up in the home of a displaced West Virginian, I was privy to a litany of maxims which my friends and peers never had the good fortune of knowing.

I remember like yesterday the time in fourth grade when I casually announced to my classmates that I was so mad I could "thread a sewing machine – and it running."

My proclamation was immediately met with a volley of hysterical laughter from everyone ranging from the teacher on down to the oddly quiet girl who sat in the back of the class and never spoke to anyone – looking back, it still makes my ears turn red with embarrassment to think that I actually "cast my pearls before the swine" in such a manner.

I remember well the feeling of nervous confusion which immediately swept over my body that day as I struggled to understand why that saying brought my classmates such amusement – to me it was a common phrase, one that I had heard my father nonchalantly utter on a near-weekly basis throughout the entirety of my young life.

As I grew older, it didn't take me very long to realize that the countless number of similes and proverbs my father could quote better than the "Romans Road" were a rarity to our host-community. As a teenager, I would cringe each time I would hear him say "shaking like a cat crapping peach seeds" or proclaim that he had worked more hours that week than some mysterious man named Carter had liver pills.

While in college, I thought that I had finally cracked the mysterious saying and at last unlocked who this cryptic Carter feller with all the liver ailments actually was – it had to have been Billy Carter.

Surely you remember Billy, President Jimmy Carter's younger brother? You remember, the guy who once urinated on an airport runway... in full view of the press and dignitaries? The guy who caused the 39th President of the United States more PR problems than... I'll spare you the pun!

After all, Billy Carter was the proud promoter of Billy Beer, so surely, of all people named Carter, he had to have had the most liver pills.

So for the next decade, each time I would hear my Dad declare that some woman had more wrinkles than Carter had liver pills, just after announcing that she could probably land a job "hainting houses," I would silently pat myself on the back, glorifying in my own intellect for finally solving this terrible riddle.

Sadly, I was recently forced into the heartbreaking realization that I did not know what I thought I knew when it comes to Appalachian etymology. Reading a yellow and tattered newspaper from the 1800s earlier this week, my jaw nearly dropped to the ground when I saw of all things, an advertisement for "Carter's Little Liver Pills." To steal an expression my grandmother would often use, "Why you could have knocked me over with a feather."

Turns out, long before Mr. Billy Carter ever tasted his first drop of alcohol, another Carter had liver pills.

The real Carter was a man from Erie, Pennsylvania, named Samuel J. Carter. In 1868, he began peddling a pill he said could cure any type of stomach sickness, marketing them as "Carter's Little Liver Pills."

Within a generation, the pills were being touted to cure, everything from headaches to constipation and indigestion.

In 2000, after racking up nearly 78% of the vote against Republican challenger David T. Gallaher, U.S. Senator Robert Byrd announced to jubilant supporters that "West Virginia has always had four friends, God Almighty, Sears Roebuck, Carter's Liver Pills and Robert C. Byrd."

So take pride West Virginia. We've got more things going for us than Carter's got liver pills!

Stories from Kentucky

The Heartbreaking Story of Jenny Wiley

Appalachian Magazine Staff

Born in Pennsylvania, around the year 1760, Jenny Sellards was nothing out of the ordinary. Her father, Hezekiah Sellards, was without wealth and the family's early years were filled with struggles.

Sellards eventually moved his family to Walker's Creek in what is now Bland County, Virginia. It was there in 1778 that Jenny met and married Thomas Wiley, a young Irish immigrant.

Soon afterward, the couple built a log cabin and had their first four children.

Alone on the frontier, young Jenny could never have imagined the events that awaited her in the days to come.

On October 1, 1789, Thomas set out for a trading post with a horse heavy laden with ginseng — an early form of currency for mountain settlers in the Appalachia. He hoped to use the ginseng to barter for his family's domestic necessities prior to the onset of winter.

That same afternoon, Jenny's brother-in-law, John Borders, heard owl-call signals in the woods which made him

Photo: Jenny Wiley's Grave in River, Kentucky

suspect Native Americans were in the area and planning an attack. He warned his sister-in-law to pack up her children and leave the cabin, but Jenny wanted to finish some household chores before leaving and made the life altering decisions to remain behind.

Not long after Borders had departed, a group of eleven Native Americans, comprised of two Cherokees, three Shawnees, three Wyandots, and three Delawares attempted to storm the cabin. Jenny and her younger brother heard the Native Americans coming and tried to barricade the door, fighting for their lives.

Sadly, their defenses was futile, as the attackers killed Jenny's younger brother, who was only fifteen-years-old.

In addition to killing her brother, the Native Americans also killed all of her children except her youngest, a two-year-old.

Expecting her fifth child, Jenny and her two-year-old were taken captive and driven westward toward Kentucky.

As the entourage moved westward, there was some dispute among her captives regarding what to do with Jenny and her young baby — as the two were slowing the party down as they made their retreat deeper into the young nation's wilderness.

Eventually deciding to spare their lives, the band of murderers continued through the Appalachian Mountains until the young child became desperately ill — it was at this point that the captors killed the baby while Jenny slept.

Sometime later, Jenny gave birth to the child she had been carrying, however, her hellish kidnappers immediately seized the child and began to play a gruesome and murderous game.

Placing the newborn onto a piece of wood, the demonically charged warriors decreed that if the child would cry they would scalp it alive, but if the newborn infant remained silent, they would permit it to live.

Sadly, the child cried almost instantly and — true to their word — the wicked alliance immediately began scalping the young baby.

Jenny was held captive by Native Americans for several additional months in what is presently Little Mud Lick Creek, Johnson County, Kentucky.

In the midst of a terrible rain storm, Jenny managed to successfully flee from the Indian camp, escaping to a nearby trading post.

Local settlers at the trading post assisted her in making her way back to Walker's Creek and her husband, who had remained faithfully remained hopeful of her return.

Once home, Jenny and her husband renewed their love and began a new family.

Somewhere around the year 1800, the Wiley family crossed the Big Sandy River, and settled in what is currently Johnson County, Kentucky. Jenny and her husband, Thomas, had five additional children.

Jenny Wiley lived in Johnson County, Kentucky, with her family until her death in 1831. She was buried near the farm in River, where she spent her final years.

Chilling: Boone Helm, "The Kentucky Cannibal"

Appalachian Magazine Staff

Through- the years, the Commonwealth of Kentucky has been home to some notable individuals and characters, ranging from famed statesmen such as Henry Clay and Abraham Lincoln to famous celebrities such as Johnny Depp and Papa John; however, it's hard to imagine a more infamous Kentuckian than Lincoln County's Boone Helm.

Born in January 1828 into what was considered an honest and hardworking home, few could have imagined what the quick moving and strong as an ox young boy would grow to become.

As a teenager, Helm would goad men into fights and demonstrated a total disdain for law enforcement.

At the age of 20, Helm married a 17-year-old girl and soon fathered a daughter. Sadly, the Helm home was anything but peaceful, as the excessive drinker would often ride his horse into the family's house at a full gallop and then proceed to beat his wife.

According to historians, the domestic violence grew to such an extent that Lucinda petitioned the local court for a divorce and Helm's father actually paid for the costs of the divorce.

With his family now bankrupted and his reputation ruined, Helm became enamored by tales of the California Gold Rush and set out to make his fortune beyond the Rockies.

Initially, Helm's cousin had decided to accompany him "Out West", however, when it came time to leave, the cousin backed out, which greatly angered Helms — so much so that he pulled out his knife and stabbed the man in the chest, instantly killing him.

Helm then headed west alone.

The brother and friends of the man he murdered pursued and captured Helm, but his antics in captivity quickly landed him in an asylum for the mentally deranged. Upon entering the asylum, Helm became taciturn and convinced his guard to take him on walks through the woods. After these walks became routine, Helm was able to take advantage of the guard's trust, deceive him, and escape.

Helm then headed west to California. On the way, he murdered several men in various altercations, eventually committing premeditated murder. Forced to flee to avoid arrest and vigilante justice, Helm teamed up with six men with whom he confided that in his past Helm had eaten all or part of some of his murder victims. "Many's the poor devil I've killed, at one time or another... and the time has been that I've been obliged to feed on some of 'em." This boastful allusion is the first report of cannibalism on the part of Boone Helm.

An attack by Natives on the way to Fort Hall, Idaho, forced Helm and his party into the wilderness. Short on provisions, Helm and his remaining party killed their horses, ate the meat, and made snowshoes out of the hides. The journey was arduous, winnowing the party down to two men: Helm and a man named Burton. When Burton could go no further, Helm left him only to return in time to hear the pistol shot of Burton taking his own life.

Helm ate one of Burton's legs and wrapped the other to take with him on his journey. Someone finally discovered Helm at an Indian camp and allowed Helm to accompany him. Despite having over fourteen hundred dollars in coins on his person, Helm reportedly neither paid nor thanked this person for feeding, clothing, and transporting him to Salt Lake City.

Boone became wanted by the law and fled to San Francisco, California.

While in California Helm killed a rancher who had befriended him and taken him in, sheltering him from the vengeance of the law. Helm then traveled to Oregon and resumed robbing people for a living, frequently murdering them. In 1862 after heavy drinking Helm gunned down an unarmed man named Dutch Fred in a saloon and fled. While on the run, Helm ate another fugitive who had been accompanying him. Captured by the authorities, Helm implored his brother "Old Tex", one of Helm's twelve siblings, for assistance. With a considerable amount of money, "Old Tex" paid off all of the witnesses. Unable to convict Helm without witnesses, the authorities released him and he accompanied his brother to Texas. Helm soon reappeared at many of the settlements mentioned before, killing many more men in the process.

Finally, Helm was apprehended in Montana.

After teaming up with the notorious Henry Plummer and his gang, Helm and four other gang members were captured, arrested, and tried in secret.

At trial, Helm kissed the Bible and then proceeded to perjure himself, accusing "Three-Fingered Jack" Garner, Helm's close friend and fellow gang member of crimes Helm himself had committed.

The Montana Vigilantes hanged Helm, Gallager, and other members of the gang in Virginia City, Montana on January 14, 1864 in front of a crowd of six thousand.

Upon seeing his friend Gallager hanged, Helm reportedly remarked "Kick away old fellow. My turn next. I'll be in Hell with you in a minute."

When the executioner approached Helm, he allegedly exclaimed "Let 'er rip!" and then jumped off of the hangman's box before it could be kicked away.

The Part of Kentucky That Isn't In Kentucky!

Appalachian Magazine Staff

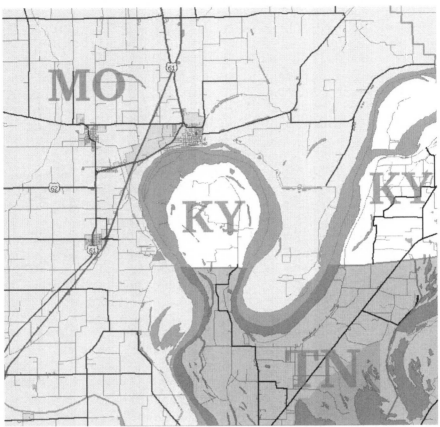

Map: Courtesy of Jim Efaw

Being the geography nerd that I am, I often find myself noticing peculiar oddities in maps that go unnoticed to most people – as was the case a couple of years ago when I came across a particular portion of extreme western Kentucky that isn't really even in Kentucky.

Known as the "Kentucky Bend," Fulton County's westernmost 17.5 square miles is only accessible from Tennessee and is separated from the county and state's mainland by the State of Missouri.

Roughly an hour's drive from the county courthouse, the land is part of Kentucky thanks to the shortsightedness of early border agreements, which established the Commonwealth of Kentucky's southwestern border as being the land north of roughly 36°29'53N that was found to lie on the eastern bank of the Mississippi River.

Surveyors marking the boundary between Kentucky and Tennessee had only estimated where their line would meet the Mississippi; later, more detailed surveys revealed the location of this line to pass directly through a series of snaking meanders of the river, effectively giving Kentucky a sizable portion of land that was north of the Tennessee line and east of the Mississippi River – even though it was west of a portion of Missouri's territory that lay on the western bank of the Great River... Yes, a little confusing, but that's what makes this story so interesting!

The result is a peninsula of land belonging to the Bluegrass State that doesn't touch Kentucky territory, is separated from its own county-seat by Missouri and is only accessible by land through Tennessee.

Lying as the farthest portion of the state downriver, the Kentucky Bend serves as the lowest point in Kentucky.

In the fall of 2013, I took a drive into this area only to discover that there isn't very much there. A simple blue "Welcome to Kentucky" sign greets motorists just beyond a typical Mississippi River shanty in what could have been a plowed cotton field.

A little farther down the road, there is a marble slab marking the spot of the Madrid Bend Families' Cemetery, which was created in 1850 and moved to its present location around 1910 due to erosion by the Mississippi River.

Outside of this, there wasn't much more to this area, which has a population of 18 individuals – it equals to be about 1 person per square mile.

Though the local residents use a Tiptonville, Tennessee, mailing address, they will earnestly contend that they are proud Kentucky residents... Something that the Volunteer State learned the hard way when they attempted to administer the area in the mid-1800s only to discover the local residents weren't about to forsake their Kentucky allegiance – even if their home state was on the other side of Missouri!

In Mark Twain's book, "Life on the Mississippi," he described the six-decade-long feud between the Darnell and Watson families, two clans who lived and brawled on this hallowed piece of Kentucky soil.

Stories from Virginia

The Polio Epidemic of Wytheville, Virginia

Appalachian Magazine Staff

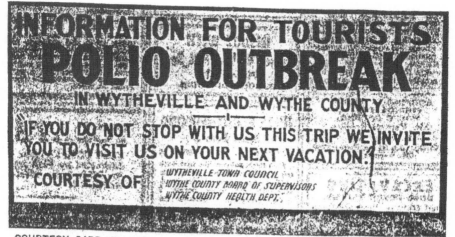

COURTESY CARD—The little town of Wytheville, Va. (pop. 5500), has set some kind of a precedent by erecting the billboard pictured above on its outskirts. This summer, Wytheville, county seat of Wythe County, suffered the worst polio epidemic in the history of the nation. Noted for its scenery, climate and vacation facilities, Wythe County was visited by thousands of tourists from all over the U. S. Wythevillians, while glad to have the visitors, did not want to take any chances on their contracting polio. Hence the sign, asking tourists to include the town in the vacation plans for next year. Health authorities state that, following this year's epidemic, Wytheville will be one of the most polio-free areas next year.

The Southwest Virginia community of Wytheville is a charming Norman Rockwell-like town. Known for its unique landmarks which include an iconic water tower painted to resemble a hot air balloon and a massive No. 2 pencil hanging over Main Street, the Town of Wytheville is the American idea of what Small Town, USA, should be.

A decade following the Second World War, however, the rural Virginia getaway community was anything but the ideal place to visit.

In the opening days of summer 1950, a handful of local citizens became infected with infantile paralysis (polio), an infectious and deadly disease that attacks the muscles of one's body.

An unfortunate characteristic with polio is that those infected with the disease can carry the infection for up to six weeks with no symptoms present — meaning that by the time the townspeople began showing signs of polio, it was too late. By the end of July, Danville, Virginia's The Bee, reported, that at least 65 residents of Wytheville (population 5,500), had been infected with the disease. Roughly 20 additional Wythe County residents – living past the town limits – were struck with polio, bringing the community's total number of polio cases to 84 at month's end.

"There are signs that Wytheville's virulent outbreak of polio — the worst in the nation — is spreading," reported the Associated Press.

Sensing the danger of a nationwide pandemic, health officials from the Commonwealth of Virginia were dispatched to the area, where they called for a "voluntary effort to keep persons from uninfected areas away from Wytheville and adjacent counties."

Their calls were heeded, as local churches cancelled services and the town's Class D Blue Ridge League baseball team cancelled the remainder of their season.

The Town Council and county's Board of Supervisors erected billboards at all five entrances to the county warning potential visitors of the epidemic and urging tourists to come again the following year.

Residents who lived east of the town, along the banks of Reed Creek, feared touching the water that flowed from Wytheville.

"People were scared out of their minds," remembered one local resident who was just a young girl at the time. "My dad warned us that if we'd go near the creek we'd probably die."

At the conclusion of summer, the town of 5,513 residents had 184 inhabitants who had contracted the disease with 17 fatalities.

As the epidemic progressed, ambulances drove victims approximately 80 miles to Memorial Crippled Children's Hospital in Roanoke, Virginia. Hearses from local funeral homes were used when ambulances were unavailable. Black patients with polio were repeatedly denied admission to Roanoke's hospital and were forced to travel approximately 300 miles to St. Philip's Hospital in Richmond.

Just as quickly as the dreaded disease appeared, it disappeared. In the years ahead, the quaint rural Virginia community would return to being the tourist getaway it is celebrated to be today — but you'll be hard pressed to find a lifelong resident of Wytheville over the age of 70 who won't remember the Polio Epidemic of 1950.

The Wytheville, Va. Woman Who Became America's "Secret President" in 1919

Appalachian Magazine Staff

Born during reconstruction in the former Confederate stronghold of Wytheville, Virginia, Edith Bolling seemed about as unlikely a candidate to serve as America's "Secret President" following a major world war at the time of her birth as anyone around; however, thanks to marrying well and a few strokes of dumb luck, the Southwest Virginia-born woman had successfully maneuvered her way not only into the White House, but as the defacto head of the country by the fall of 1919.

Through her father, Bolling was a direct descendant of Pocahontas and prior to the American Civil War, the family was said to have been quite wealthy – owning both a large plantation as well as several slaves; however, at war's end, the Confederate sympathizing family was left nearly destitute and Edith's father was forced to settle on his father's property in Wytheville, where he became the county's judge.

As she grew older, Edith received very little formal education — a semester at Martha Washington College and then she enrolled in Powell's

School for Girls in Richmond for a year.

A short while later, Edith married Norman Galt, a prominent Washington, D.C., jeweler she had met while visiting her sister in the nation's capital.

Sadly, only twelve years into their marriage, Galt died unexpectedly, leaving Edith a widow at the age of 35.

In March 1915, the widow Edith was introduced to widower US President Woodrow Wilson at the White House by Helen Woodrow Bones, the president's first cousin and official White House hostess since the death of First Lady Ellen Wilson only seven months earlier.

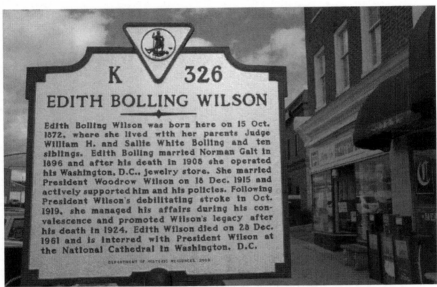

Photo: Edith Bolling Wilson birthplace in Downtown, Wytheville, Virginia

According to reports, "Wilson took an instant liking to Galt and his admiration grew swiftly into love."

The President's new found love quickly found a hungry audience in the nation's early tabloids soon rumors of the romance began to escalate.

It was not uncommon for people to state that they believed Wilson had been cheating on his first wife, or that he and Edith had actually murdered the First Lady — despite the fact that the First Lady had died following a continued battle with Bright's Disease, kidney failure.

Distressed at the effect the rumors may have been having on his new fiancée, Wilson offered Edith the opportunity to back out of their engagement, but she declined and the two were married on December 18, 1915, at her home in Washington, D.C.

The couple honeymooned two weeks in Hot Springs, Virginia and at

The Greenbrier in White Sulphur Springs, West Virginia.

Soon, the honeymoon was over and the pressing matters of state had escalated into the First World War.

Both the war and the immediate peace that followed the conflict weighed heavily upon the 62-year-old President and in October 1919, President Wilson suffered a stroke that left him partly paralyzed.

Photo: Woodrow Wilson and Edith Bolling Galt were married in this house on December 18, 1915.

With her husband paralyzed and suffering from a great stroke, Edith Bolling Wilson took over many routine duties and details of the Executive branch of the government from then until Wilson left office almost a year and a half later.

She decided which matters of state were important enough to bring to the bedridden president.

"I studied every paper sent from the different Secretaries or Senators," she wrote later of her role, "and tried to digest and present in tabloid form the things that, despite my vigilance, had to go to the President. I, myself, never made a single decision regarding the disposition of public affairs. The only decision that was mine was what was important and what was not, and the very important decision of when to present matters to my husband."

Despite her assurances that she did not make any decisions, no one could say for certain, as the ailing President was closely guarded.

One Republican senator labeled her "the Presidentress who had fulfilled the dream of the suffragettes by changing her title from First Lady to Acting First Man."

In My Memoir, published in 1939, she called her role a "stewardship" and insisted that her actions had been taken only because the president's doctors told her to do so for her husband's mental health.

Some historians, however, have taken issue with her version of events, such as journalist Phyllis Lee Levin.

She wrote that Edith Wilson was "a woman of narrow views and formidable determination."

In contrast, Wilson's chief of staff Joe Tumulty wrote "No public man ever had a more devoted helpmeet, and no wife a husband more dependent

Photo: President Wilson and First Lady Edith Bolling Galt Wilson.

upon her sympathetic understanding of his problems...Mrs. Wilson's strong physical constitution, combined with strength of character and purpose, has sustained her under a strain which must have wrecked most women."

In March 1921, President Wilson and First Lady Edith moved out of the White House and into a Washington, D.C. townhouse where he attempted to restore his health; sadly, the former President died on February 3, 1924, at home of a stroke and other heart-related problems.

The day following the Japanese Attack on Pearl Harbor, when President Roosevelt appeared before Congress, asking for a declaration of War, he was accompanied by the former First Lady.

Edith Bolling Wilson stayed in their D.C. home for the remainder of her life, dying there at the age 89 on December 28, 1961, which would have been Woodrow Wilson's 105th birthday.

Downtown Wytheville now showcases the life of Mrs. Edith Bolling Wilson at the Edith Bolling Wilson Birthplace Museum, just across the street from the Bolling-Wilson Hotel.

Lee County: Virginia's Most Western County

Appalachian Magazine Staff

Photo: Lee County, Virginia, Courtesy of Albert Herring

Geographically positioned farther west than the city of Detroit, Virginia's Lee County stands as the Old Dominion's westernmost locality and has for centuries acted as a bridge for pioneers desiring to forsake the lifestyle of the East for the untouched wilderness beyond the Cumberland Gap.

Deep in the heart of this historic county, which dates back to October 1792, is its westernmost community of Ewing, Virginia.

Farther west than West Virginia's westernmost point, this Virginia hamlet is a far cry from the metropolises that sit at the other ends of the Commonwealth. While places such as Virginia Beach and Fairfax boast of areas with just about as many people per square mile as the entire County of Lee, Ewing acts as the state's most distant community and offers a plethora of oddities for the history and geography nerd.

Defined as a census-designated place, Ewing has a population of roughly 439 residents, however, what this borderline Midwestern community lacks in size it makes up for with intriguing stories.

Dating back to around the time this community first got a post office in 1891, the mountains and valleys surrounding the settlement have played host to a number of murders and murderers.

In the spring of 1901, Lee County's former sheriff, Charles M. Edds, was put on trial for the murder of his brother-in-law, Charles Ball, a serving sheriff's deputy.

According to the Richmond Times, "There had been an old grudge between them for about three years."

A Louisville paper from the previous November detailed the murder:

"Ball was assassinated... near Ewing, Virginia, while on his way from Cumberland Gap... He was found a few days after his death by the roadside with eight bullet holes in his body. Edds was last seen with him and was suspected."

Despite the evidence against him, the former sheriff managed to convince eight of the twelve jurors of his innocence and was subsequently acquitted.

The region was again the scene of bloodshed only a handful of years later. The November 10, 1905, edition of the Hartford Republican speaks about troops being stationed at the border of Virginia, Kentucky and Tennessee, as a band of outlaws, under the leadership of Riley Ball, "a sixteen-year-old boy," exercised sovereignty over the forgotten land.

Though the advent of push button communication, planes, trains and automobiles have all worked to bring this forgotten territory a little closer to the government-seat in charge of her, the reality is that no invention of man can erase the fact that this Virginia town is geographically closer to nine state capitals than her very own in Richmond, which is more than 410 miles away.

Closer capitals are: Frankfort, KY (178 miles), Charleston, WV (216 miles), Nashville, TN (240 miles), Atlanta, GA (264 miles), Columbia, SC (301 miles), Columbus, OH (322 miles), Indianapolis, IN (322 miles), Raleigh, NC (331 miles), and Montgomery, AL (407 miles).

TEXAS: A Creation of Appalachia

Appalachian Magazine Staff

According to his own account, after losing re-election, the great Appalachian Congressman Davy Crockett angrily told his Tennessee constituents "You may all go to hell and I will go to Texas."

Making good on his promise, Crockett said goodbye to the Volunteer State in the fall of 1835 with three other men and headed into the vast wonderland of Texas.

His youngest child, Matilda, later wrote that she distinctly remembered the last time she saw her father, "He was dressed in his hunting suit, wearing a coonskin cap, and carried a fine rifle presented to him by friends in Philadelphia ... He seemed very confident the morning he went away that he would soon have us all to join him in Texas."

Born in what is now Greene County, Tennessee, Crockett was the son of Scots-Irish mountaineers who settled the rugged region of Western Carolina and East Tennessee, and they did so on purpose. In those days, the steep Appalachian Mountains that cut through the young nation honored rugged individualism and placed miles between its inhabitants and the ruling authorities back east. Life in those mountains was hard and men were their own law — exactly as they would have it to be.

In his first campaign for Congress, Crockett found himself in a debate with his opponent, a learned and slick orator who was discussing issues concerning tariffs and the national bank. "Crockett knew little or nothing about either subject, but he was in no wise disconcerted. When it came his turn to speak, he made a few friendly remarks, then asked his all-male audience if they would like to wet their whistles. Their response was said to have been a spontaneous and cordial 'Yes.' It was Crockett who won the election," writes Fred DeArmond.

Unfortunately for the mountain man turned politician, by the 1830s, even the once free and untamed Appalachian Mountains had begun to show the early signs of being tamed — or at the very least captured. A reality that was only reinforced when the influx of new Tennesseeans selected a refined criminal-lawyer over Mr. Crockett as their representative to Congress.

What was a free spirited Scotsman left to do?

The same as his grandparents had done two generations earlier: Go west in search of that final frontier. That final holdout of individualism and in the mid-1830s Texas was that place.

In the days ahead, Crockett and a host of other men would find their way into Texas mythology when they gave their lives defending a remote mission that would come to be known simply as "The Alamo". The event marked a turning point in the Texas Revolution and served as a rallying cry that would soon lead to the creation of the Republic of Texas.

Among the men who fought alongside Crockett at the Battle of the Alamo, 17 were Virginians, 30 were from Tennessee, 17 from Kentucky and 14 were from the Carolinas.

However, the sons of Appalachia were busy paving the way for the Lonestar State long before Santa Anna and the war for Texas Independence.

Stephen F. Austin, the man who secured his title in history as the "Father of Texas" was born on the banks of the New River in the Blue Ridge Mountains of western Virginia in 1793.

According to local historians, Austin's father and uncle were "excellent shot makers and miners, but they were not very good businessmen."

Burdened by debt, the brothers are said to have looked westward, beyond the mountains of their home.

Nearly two decades later, the Austin's relocated to the largely unsettled expanse of Texas.

Stephen's father had hopes of colonizing the region in the days ahead, however, he died in 1821 having never realized his dream of settling the vast territory known as "Tejas."

Persuaded by a letter from his mother, Wythe County, Virginia, native Stephen F. Austin set out to fulfill his father's dream: settle Texas.

Under Austin's leadership, the Texas colony grew from three-hundred to over 11,000 by 1832.

Soon the colonists found themselves in a state of war with the Mexican government and rushing to their aid were men of the mountains.

After the dust had finally settled and Texans went to the polls to elect their first President, Rockbridge County, Virginia, native and Tennessee lawyer Sam Houston beat out the New River Valley's Stephen F. Austin for the office.

In the face of continuing hardship and increasingly authoritative governments in the east, a countless number of mountaineers would say goodbye to the Appalachians and follow in the footsteps of Crocket, Bowie, Austin and Houston.

"Gone to Texas" became a wellknown phrase throughout the mountains during the 1800s as farmers, miners and a host of other working men would simply paint "GTT" on the front doors of their abandonded homes and fenceposts to let everyone know they had "Gone to Texas".

In his top selling book American Nations: A History of the Eleven Rival Regional Cultures of North America, Colin Woodard traces the common culture, ethinc origin, dialect, artifacts and symbols of the various people groups that originally settled America and the Greater Appalachian influence stretches from Central Virginia to far-eastern New Mexico, engulfing West Texas, Texas Panhandle and central regions of the state.

If you've ever noticed similarities in the folks from Texas and Appalachia, it's largely because they're one in the same.

Photo: Stephen F. Austin Birthplace Monument, Austinville, Virginia

Virginia & West Virginia's Shared Tunnel

Appalachian Magazine Staff

Photo: East River Mountain Tunnel portal on the Virginia side. Courtesy, benuski

When the God of Creation molded the landscapes of eastern and western Virginia, He erected a mountain barrier between the two regions that helped to fuel an intra-state dispute which ended only when the two incompatible sections were under the authorities of different state governments.

While Western Virginia's chief geographic features are tall and long mountain ridges with lush and wide valleys in between, the Mountain State's geography features countless steep mountains splotched together in an elaborate prehistoric maze.

For centuries, this great divide has worked to create two unique and totally different cultures in the Virginias. One whose history was made by farmers and statesmen and another that has been defined by coal mining and labor wars.

This contrast between the two states is one that continues even unto this day: since 1968, Virginia and West Virginia have voted differently in 8 of the past 12 presidential elections. For years, West Virginia was a Democratic stronghold, whereas Virginia chose the Republican candidate for president in every election from 1964 to 2004. Interestingly, as West Virginia's Republicans have found new success in Charleston, the Commonwealth's Democrats have successfully transformed the Old Dominion into a blue state on a national level... It seems that the two states simply have to be different!

A major step was taken to bring the two sides of the mountain together, however, in the summer of 1969.

While the rest of the world was crinking their necks, trying to spot Neil Armstrong dancing about the moon, workers in Mercer County, West Virginia, and Bland County, Virginia, were fixated upon the 3,584-ft. tall East River Mountain, the border between Virginia and West Virginia.

Over the next several years, the two states invested over $40 MILLION in blasting through the bedrock of the mountain, creating two separate tunnels through wall of earth, in an effort to pave the way for President Eisenhower's envisioned Interstate – 77, linking Cleveland, Ohio, to Columbia, South Carolina.

"The work was difficult, the TNT explosions were loud and the mud was deep. At East River Mountain, caves created sinkholes and sunk part of the tunnel two feet so that concrete had to be hauled in to correct the problem. More than 30,000 feet of lumber was also hauled in to support the tunnel," wrote Rickie Longfellow.

Photo: Construction on the East River Mountain Tunnel

Construction on the East River Mountain Tunnel

Work on the twin 5,400 ft. tunnels through the mountain was officially completed at a ribbon-cutting ceremony on December 20, 1974. The tunnel carries the biggest price tag of any project done to date by the West Virginia Department of Highways.

Roughly midway through the tunnel, an observant motorist will find a green sign, stating "STATE LINE: WV / VA." The East River Mountain Tunnel is one of only two instances in the United States where a mountain road tunnel crosses a state line. The other is the Cumberland Gap Tunnel, connecting Tennessee and Kentucky.

For Virginia, the $40 MILLION East River Mountain Tunnel was just a portion of the costs associated with Interstate 77. Roughly 20 miles to the south of the East

Photo: Inside the East River Mountain Tunnel, Courtesy of US Dept. of Transportation, FHA

River Mountain Tunnel is the Big Walker Mountain Tunnel, near the border of Bland and Wythe County, Virginia. The Big Walker Mountain Tunnel carried a price tag of $50 MILLION and was the most expensive single project undertaken on Virginia's interstate system at the time.

Each day, tens of thousands of motorists pass through the two tunnels, which are roughly 15-minute apart. According to the Beckley Post Herald, the East River Mountain Tunnel alone has cut the travel time from Wytheville to Beckley in half.

For those like me, who love the cultures and people residing on both sides of the mountain, we can only imagine how drastically different things would be today had this tunnel been created a little more than a century earlier.

Stories from West Virginia

Titanic: Made with West Virginia Timber

Appalachian Magazine Staff

Despite being branded as 'wild and wonderful,' the sad reality is that West Virginia's present-day forests are but a frail shell of what was once a majestic and unimaginably dense woodland — a vast and mysterious expanse which both sweetened and haunted the dreams of many early settlers.

One of the earliest men to write of the state's ancient forests was a surveyor by the name of George Washington.

On November 4, 1770, while plotting the Kanawha River, he wrote in his journal, "Just as we came to the hills, we met with a Sycamore... of a most extraordinary size, it measuring three feet from the ground, forty-five feet round, lacking two inches; and not fifty yards from it was another, thirty-one feet round."

Bill Grafton, president of the West Virginia Native Plant Society stated, "In Pre-Colonial times, the 15 million acres of West Virginia were almost entirely forested."

The trees, centuries-old colossal mammoths, towered proudly over the Mountain State — standing like skyscrapers of the ancient world, reigning for thousands of years over the majestic and unconquerable land. Older than the Mayflower, many of West Virginia's white oak and hemlock trees were more than half-a-millennium old – an unimaginable spectacle for the European colonists who first laid eyes on the trees.

As their Native American predecessors who first inhabited the land, the early colonists who topped the mountain ridges which had protected the enchanted land for ages, lacked the resources or will to destroy the hallowed trees of old.

Unfortunately, within a few generations, the western world had been thrust into an era which came to be known as the Industrial Revolution; soon, man's appetite for tangible goods had reached a level that had previously been unthinkable.

Seeking to profit from society's thirst for stuff, sawmills sprang up throughout the mountains of the newly created state, as armies of rough, strong and desperate men set out, hewing down the ancient landmarks of old. The workers themselves were not villains, but immigrants, laborers, husbands and fathers of hungry children; unaware of their own strength.

By 1920, the state, which is now celebrated for its natural beauty, had been reduced to an abhorrent desert, more closely resembling a bombed wasteland than a mountain wonderland described as being "almost heaven."

For the first time in its history, West Virginia was viewed as an eyesore. One visiting writer described the state as "a monotonous panorama of destruction."

Recognizing the dangers wrought by absentee landownership and unregulated devouring of the state's forests, West Virginia leaders would move, in the coming years, to reforest the mountains which lay between the Old Dominion and the Ohio River.

By 2000, their efforts had been deemed a success, as the state had reforested itself and boasted of more forestland than it had seen in over a century.

Though the era of rampant deforestation is a major blight in the magnificent state's history, the undeniable reality is that West Virginia's trees were the building material of America as we know it. With a single tree yielding over 10,000 oak boards, it would be impossible to determine the number of churches, home places, courthouses and ships which were made from West Virginia lumber. One thing we are certain about, however, is that the 46,328-ton HMS Titanic, which sank to the bottom of the North Atlantic on April 15, 1912, carried with it sawed planks of the giant tree pictured above — hewed down in Nicolas County, West Virginia.

West Virginia is a proud state, and by right ought to be — for no other state can boast of having literally made America, and modern-day Western Civilization, as West Virginia can.

62

The Canal That Could Have Saved "Western" Virginia

Appalachian Magazine Staff

Out of all the early colonies, the only state whose geography created a conundrum that could even be comparable to Virginia's was that of the State of New York.

Though not nearly as formidable as the Blue Ridge, New York's Adirondack Mountains effectively separate large portions of the state from its eastern commercial hub.

Fearful that such a division would prove to be a cause for fracture, the solution devised by state leaders was to build a canal that would enable navigation from New York City to the state's capital city of Albany and then to the state's far western boundary at Buffalo.

With construction beginning on July 4, 1817, the Erie Canal was finally completed on October 26, 1825.

Constructing the 363-mile system cost $7million and has been hailed as one of the greatest engineering marvels of the nineteenth century.

Though pricey, historians make the case that the canal may have saved New York from the same fragmentation Virginia experienced, as well as helped to solidify New York City as the world's center for commerce and trade.

An even more audacious undertaking by early Virginia leaders was the James River & Kanawha Canal.

The plan, which was originally surveyed by George Washington, was begun in 1785.

Intended to facilitate shipments of passengers and freight by water between the western counties of Virginia and the coast, the expensive project suffered numerous setbacks due to a lack in funding, flood damage and the sheer climb in elevation from the coastal sea level to the headwaters of the New River.

Though largely financed by the Commonwealth of Virginia through the Virginia Board of Public Works, it was only half completed by 1851, reaching the Town of Buchanan, in Botetourt County, roughly 60 miles from the canal's intended target, the south fork of the Kanawha, more commonly known as the New River.

The canal became an early indicator of the sectional strife the two regions would find themselves a party to in the years ahead, as Virginia General Assembly records from 1829-30 reveal.

Commenting on this early dispute, James McGregor wrote:

"The western members of the convention were accused of making an attempt to swamp the state with a debt created for the purpose of benefiting the west alone."

Most noteworthy, however, is that the greatest opposition to the

Photo: James River Canal near intersection of Blue Ridge Parkway at Battery Creek Appalachian Magazine.

public works project came from leaders in the Western Virginia's Northern Panhandle and other communities of the state's northern region. Those in the north of what would become West Virginia were in favor of a canal linking the Ohio River to the Chesapeake Bay, as it would allow them additional opportunities to do business with the cities of Baltimore and

Washington.

"Of far greater importance to the state was the project which had for its purpose the connecting of the James and the Kanawha rivers. Here the benefits would have been far greater to the Richmond district than to any western region. But lack of foresight again was the cause of the failure of the plan, which might have prevented in 1861 the defection of the counties drained by the Kanawha. Thus the golden opportunity was allowed to slip by with but feeble attempts to carry out the projected scheme, and when the Civil War broke out the canal had been completed only as far as the town of Buchanan."

Photo: Remnants of James River Canal near intersection of Blue Ridge Parkway. Appalachian Magazine.

In an annual report, one Virginia delegate implored his colleagues to lay aside all petty jealousies and pass a bill for the union of the James and the Kanawha rivers, "and thus complete one of the grandest schemes that has engaged the attention of the country since the proposition of the Erie Canal."

Unfortunately, lack in financing and the rise of rail transportation rendered the James River & Kanawha Canal too costly to continue and the program was scrapped in the town of Buchanan – having never left the James River watershed. Had the canal been successful in pushing through the Blue Ridge Mountains and into the Kanawha River's Drainage Basin, Western Virginians would have had a straight and navigable passageway to Virginia's Capital City of Richmond and the disunion felt by so many in the mountains of Western Virginia may never had existed — just sixty miles and the entire outcome of the American Civil War may have been altered.

Logan, West Virginia:
Once a Native American Capital City
Appalachian Magazine Staff

The year was 1756. Finding themselves in a bitter and savage war against the French, Britain mustered thousands of regular soldiers to what was at the time, the very end of the civilized world.

Their mission was simple – make contact with and drive out enemy forces along the Ohio Valley.

The fate of the war would ultimately determine the future of the North American continent — had the English lost this conflict, the people of West Virginia would undoubtedly be speaking French today.

Among the many thousands of square miles of land up for grabs was the region that surrounded the Guyandotte River.

Named for Henry Guyan, a French trader who made the first settlement in the region six years earlier, the Guyandotte River's territory was a French stronghold.

Soon, a series of bloody mountain battles would test the resolve of England's most well trained fighting men.

With Virginia's western frontier a hundred miles to their southeast, the Redcoats found themselves fighting the first of what would soon be many full-fledged military battles on the North American continent.

Unfortunately for them, they would quickly find that unlike the gentlemen engagements of Europe, the rules and ways of war in the New World would be unlike anything the British had previously seen.

Trained to wage war on the open pasturelands of Europe, with rows of disciplined soldiers standing resolute awaiting a volley of enemy bullets, Britain's Redcoats were unprepared for mountain warfare.

Among the thousands of English soldiers fighting against a phantom enemy hidden within the virgin forests of the Appalachian Mountains was a soldier named Boling Baker.

Following a failed assault against a French controlled fort which ended in disaster, Baker, a half a world away from home, made the fateful decision to desert the English army.

Hundreds of miles from the nearest English settlement, Baker wandered through the mountains of what is present-day West Virginia. Though it is unclear how long Baker wandered through the dark forests of the western frontier for an unknown number of days, before eventually being taken captive by hostile bands of Shawnee Indians.

A prisoner of war, Baker was taken by his captors to Chief Cornstalk, a prominent leader of the Shawnee nation. A council was then held to determined his punishment. The council ultimately decided to make Baker run the gauntlet (two long lines of Indians armed with clubs and tomahawks).

When it came time for Baker to face his punishment, he reportedly grabbed a tomahawk from one of his bloodthirsty captors and began to fight back with a passion and courage that excited the heart of Chief Cornstalk's sixteen-year-old daughter Aracoma.

A princess among her people, Aracoma successfully convinced her father to spare the life of the fugitive English soldier.

The two fell so deeply in love that Baker chose to forsake his English ways and convert to the Shawnee lifestyle.

After a period of trial, Cornstalk gave Baker his daughter to wed.

Their wedding ceremony lasted for three days and was filled with dancing, bonfires (which may have more closely resembled forest fires) and feasting.

As a present to his young daughter, Cornstalk gave her a tribe of Indians to rule in "a wonderful land in the heart of the forest."

Aracoma established the capitol of her tribe on an island lying in the center of the Guyandotte River, known today as both Hatfield Island and Midelburg Island.

During the Revolutionary War, American militiamen made capturing the island a top priority, due to the fact that Aracoma and her husband were using the land to stage a series of horse thefts from settlers along the New River. The island has been controlled by white men ever since.

In 1852, settlers organized the town of Aracoma on the site of the Indian settlement. Years later, the city changed its name to Logan and the rest is, as they say, history.

Today, the island is owned by Logan County, West Virginia, and has been home to the local high school since the 1957-58 school year.

Stories from
Tennessee & Carolina

Why Tennessee is Called the "Volunteer State"

Appalachian Magazine Staff

Few state nicknames are as timeless as that of Tennessee's, The Volunteer State.

The title is etched into the state's license plates, known throughout the nation, and on game day may be spotted on the fronts of approximately 102,455 bright orange t-shirts on the streets of downtown Knoxville... but what the heck does it mean? Why is Tennessee called The Volunteer State?

Like so many other aspects of history, there is fierce debate regarding this subject. But one thing is for certain – it is because of the willingness of the state's residents to volunteer for military service.

Some historians claim that the state became known as the "Volunteer State," during the War of 1812 because of prominent role the state's volunteer soldiers played in thwarting England's plans to cripple America, especially during the Battle of New Orleans.

Though this is a compelling story, especially when on considers that Tennessean Andrew Jackson, "Ole Hickory" himself, was the commander of American volunteers during this epic battle, most who have studied the subject have reached a different conclusion. According to the Columbia Encyclopedia, the nickname was given to the state during the Mexican–American War, during the late 1840s.

In the decade leading up to this war, scores of Tennesseans painted GTT (Gone to Texas) onto the front doors of their home and headed to the newly established Republic of Texas. Among these individuals was the American folk hero Davy Crockett.

In the election of 1835, the voters of Tennessee chose not to re-elect Crockett and in his farewell speech, he told his constituents, "you may all go to hell and I will go to Texas."

Making good on his promise, Crockett left the state and joined the thousands of other Appalachian-Americans who had made the move to Texas.

Sadly, the larger than life American frontiersman would eventually be killed while defending the Alamo.

Though the voters had rejected him, the people of Tennessee never forgot Crockett, nor did they ever forget the Alamo.

Roughly a decade later, the opportunity to avenge the life of Crockett and so many others against the Mexican government presented itself when Mexican General Mariano Arista was ordered to push American troops back across the Nueces River. These troops then attacked American soldiers, killing 12 American troops and taking 52 prisoners.

According to Tennessee History, future President, General Zachary Taylor, dispatched a report to President Polk saying 'hostilities had begun.

Photo: Drawing of the Alamo Mission in San Antonio. It was first printed in 1854 in Gleason's Pictorial Drawing Room

The report reached President Polk while he was dining and the President immediately called his cabinet into an emergency session.

The following week, a divided Congress agreed that a state of war existed with Mexico.

"U.S. Navy Ships immediately moved to blockade the Gulf of Mexico and others in the Pacific moved towards California ports. With a regular standing army of only 8,000 men and General Taylor screaming for reinforcements, President Polk was forced to call upon the states to raise 2,600 men each to supply the American Army in Mexico," stated Tennessee History.

The proclamation went out from Nashville that the federal government needed 2,600 volunteers to assist in the war with Mexico... Within a week's time, more than 30,000 Tennesseans responded to the call to arms. And it was from this overwhelming show of patriotism that the State of Tennessee not only assisted in winning the outright sovereignty of the State of Texas, but also in securing its lasting title as The Volunteer State.

Over a half-century later, the title was solidified in 1902, when the Atlanta Constitution dubbed the University of Tennessee's athletic team, "The Volunteers" following a football game against the Georgia Tech Yellow Jackets. Three years later, the Knoxville Journal and Tribune began using this name to describe the state's flagship university's athletic teams.

Now, the Tennessee Volunteers are just as much a part of Tennessee as Davy Crockett... who moved to Texas!

The Republic of Franklin: Appalachia's Lost Country

Appalachian Magazine Staff

In the days following the American Revolution, the united States found themselves deeply in debt from the heavy price of conducting a full-out military war with the British Empire.

Though the States had successfully secured their political independence, the economic burden felt in the thirteen statehouses scattered along the East Coast made many question whether the struggling nation would make it out of infancy.

In an effort to help the struggling nation repay war debts, the State of North Carolina voted "to give Congress the 29,000,000 acres lying between the Allegheny Mountains (as the entire Appalachian range was then called) and the Mississippi River" in April 1784

In essence, the Tarheel State agreed to give the United States Congress all of what would become the State of Tennessee –back then known simply as North Carolina's Washington District.

Carolina leaders may not have been totally pure in their motivations, however, as the vast expanse of land was proving too costly for the state to govern – Though the British had prohibited Indian settlements east of the Appalachians and white settlements west of the mountains, an estimated 30,000 settlers had moved to this area by 1784 and frequent skirmishes with local Indian tribes was becoming all too frequent.

According to historian John A. Caruso, these developments were not welcomed by the frontiersmen, who had pushed even further westward, gaining a foothold on the western Cumberland River at Fort Nashborough (now Nashville), or the Overmountain Men, many of whom had settled in the area during the days of the old Watauga Republic. Inhabitants of the region feared that the cash-starved federal Congress might even be desperate enough to sell the frontier territory to a competing foreign power such as France or Spain.

Within a matter of months, a newly elected North Carolina Legislature opted not to gift the expanse of land to the Congress, choosing instead to develop the land as marketable real estate on a vast scale.

In his book, "History of Western North Carolina," John Preston writes, "The North Carolina lawmakers ordered judges to hold court in the western counties and arranged to enroll a brigade of soldiers for defense, appointing John Sevier to form it."

Unfortunately, for the settlers of what would eventually become Tennessee, the State of North Carolina simply lacked the resources to administer such as vast territory and western pioneers quickly grew critical of the state government hundreds of miles to the east.

Feeling that his government in Richmond had neglected to protect his community, Washington County, Virginia, (far western Virginia) resident Arthur Campbell presented a plan to John Sevier: Form an entirely new state along the mountain and valley of the Appalachians.

Word of the idea quickly spread among the Overmountain towns until it eventually reached the desk of Virginia Governor Patrick Henry. Angered by the idea, Henry prompted the state's General Assembly to pass a law which forbade anyone from attempting to create a new state from the Commonwealth.

Unable to include Virginia in their plan, Campbell and Sevier pressed forward in their attempts to create a new state out of North Carolina's western frontier.

They selected to call their new state, the State of Franklin, in an attempt to solicit support from Benjamin Franklin.

The State of Franklin movement had little success on the Kentucky frontier, as settlers there wanted their own state (which they achieved in 1792).

On August 23, 1784, delegates from the North Carolina counties of Washington (which at the time included present day Carter County), Sullivan, Spencer (now Hawkins County) and Greene—all of which are in present-day Tennessee—convened in the town of Jonesborough. There, they declared the lands to be independent of the State of North Carolina.

Leaders were duly elected. John Sevier reluctantly became governor. The delegates were called to a constitutional convention held at Jonesborough in December of that year. They drafted a constitution that excluded lawyers, doctors, and preachers as candidates for election to the legislature – the constitution was defeated in referendum. Afterward, the area continued to operate under tenets of the North Carolina state constitution.

The following May a delegation submitted a petition for statehood to Congress. Eventually, seven states voted to admit what would have been the 14th federal state under the proposed name of Frankland.

This was, however, less than the two-thirds majority required under the Articles of Confederation to add additional states to the confederation. The following month, the Franklin government convened to address their options. In an attempt to curry favor for their cause, Sevier tried to persuade Franklin to support their cause by letter, but he declined, writing:

"I am sensible of the honor which your Excellency and your council thereby do me. But being in Europe when your State was formed, I am too little acquainted with the circumstances to be able to offer you anything just now that may be of importance, since everything material that regards your welfare will doubtless have occurred to yourselves. ... I will endeavor to inform myself more perfectly of your affairs by inquiry and searching the records of Congress and if anything should occur to me that I think may be useful to you, you shall hear from me thereupon." — Benjamin Franklin, Letter to Governor John Sevier, 1787

Still upset with North Carolina over taxation, protection, and other issues, leaders in Franklin began operating as a de facto independent republic after the failed statehood attempt.

Greeneville was declared the new capital. The first legislature met in Greeneville in December 1785. The delegates adopted a permanent constitution, known as the Holston Constitution, which was modeled closely upon that of North Carolina. John Sevier also proposed to commission a Franklin state flag, but it was never designed.

Franklin opened courts, incorporated and annexed five new counties and fixed taxes and officers' salaries.

The Republic's primary currency was barter with anything in common use among the people allowed in payment to settle debts, including corn, tobacco, apple brandy, and skins. (Sevier was often paid in deer hides.) Federal or foreign currencies were accepted. All citizens were granted a two-year reprieve on paying taxes, but the lack of hard currency and economic infrastructure slowed development and often created confusion.

By 1786 the tiny Appalachian State was nearing its final demise. Because they were claiming to be an independent republic, neither the federal army or the North Carolina militia served to protect the settlers from increasing Indian attacks.

In late 1786, North Carolina offered to waive all back taxes if Franklin would reunite with its government. When this offer was popularly rejected in 1787, North Carolina moved in with troops under the leadership of Col. John Tipton and re-established its own courts, jails, and government at Jonesborough.

The September 1787 meeting of the Franklin legislature, however, was its last.

At the end of 1787, loyalties were divided among the area's residents, and came to a head in early February 1788. Jonathan Pugh, the North Carolina sheriff of Washington County was ordered by the county court to seize any property of Sevier's to settle tax debts North Carolina contended was owed to them. The property seized included several slaves, who were brought to Tipton's home and secured in his underground kitchen. On February 27, Governor Sevier arrived at the Tipton house leading a force numbering more than 100 men. During a heavy snowstorm in the early morning of February 29, Colonel George Maxwell arrived with a force equivalent to Sevier's to reinforce Tipton. After ten minutes of skirmishing, Sevier and his force withdrew to Jonesborough. A number of men were captured or wounded on both sides, and three men killed.

Following the battle, Sevier attempted to form an alliance with the Spanish government. Opposed to any foreign nation gaining a foothold in Franklin, North Carolina officials arrested Sevier in August 1788. Sevier's supporters quickly freed him from the local jail and retreated to "Lesser Franklin".

In February 1789, Sevier, and the last holdouts of the "Lost State," swore oaths of allegiance to North Carolina after turning themselves in. North Carolina sent their militia to aid in driving out the Cherokee and Chickasaw.

Ultimately, however, John Sevier succeeded in seeing the mountains that he loved so dearly free from North Carolina rule. On September 23, 1803, Sevier was sworn in as the State of Tennessee's first governor.

What You May Not Have Known About Pilot Mountain

Appalachian Magazine Staff

Photo: Pilot Mountain, courtesy of Berean Hunter

Western North Carolina is home to a countless number of unique and incredible mountains, but it's hard to imagine a more recognizable or unique landform than Surry County's Pilot Mountain.

Comprised almost entirely of metamorphic quartzite, the oddly shaped pinnacle was formed thanks to the eroding away of less durable rocks surrounding the pinnacle. The result: an unmistakable land feature that now stands 1,400 feet above the immediate landscape and a millennia old beacon for wandering travelers.

An age old landmark

Long before Europeans ever arrived in the New World, the Saura Indians (also known as the Cheraw people) called the Appalachian Mountains of North Carolina home. With tribal territory stretching from present-day Galax, Virginia, to Myrtle Beach, South Carolina, the Saura were accustomed to traveling great distances and the easily distinguishable knob of Pilot Mountain helped guide them along their journeys. It is for this reason that the Saura Indians named the mountain "Jomeokee", meaning "great guide".

Sadly, the Saura Nation suffered many attacks throughout the late-1600s at the hands of the Iroquois Confederacy. In the decades ahead, encroachments by other Native American tribes as well as colonial settlers would eventually lead to the once great people's total extinction.

In the century that followed, white settlers found the unmistakable pinnacle to be a "great guide" and chose to name the mountain peak "Pilot Mountain", as the landmass served as a vital navigational reference point for westbound travelers.

In the early days of aviation, long before standardized navigational practices were implemented, airplane pilots used the highly visible mountain in the same manner traveling Indians had done five centuries earlier – making Pilot Mountain really live up to its name!

Deforestation Revealed a Second Pinnacle Rock

Few travelers passing below Pilot Mountain ever realize that there is actually a second pinnacle standing alongside the unmissable mountain.

Like so many other portions of Appalachia, the mid-1800s introduced a period of widespread deforestation, scarring the land for decades and leaving a panorama of barren land in its wake.

One unimaginable consequence of destroying North Carolina's virgin timber, however, was the revealing of a second "Little Pinnacle Rock".

Today, the State of North Carolina manages a trail and overlook at Little Pinnacle offering an incredible eye-level glimpse of Pilot Mountain's Big Pinnacle as well as a bird's eye view of Mount Airy, Fancy Gap Mountain and miles of Virginia farmland some 20 miles to the north.

Thomas Jefferson's Father Mapped the Area

According to North Carolina Parks, "The mountain was mapped in 1751 by Joshua Fry and Peter Jefferson, father of President Thomas Jefferson."

Their mapping paved the way for private land ownership of the area and in just six years' time, the large peak was purchased by a private individual and remained in private hands until the late-1960s.

"Mrs. J. W. Beasley, the owner of Pilot in the 1960s, and The Pilot Mountain Preservation and Park Committee worked together to make the land a public park. In 1976, the park became a National Natural Landmark," wrote Jonathan Martin.

Thanks to the generosity of Beasley, Pilot Mountain became North Carolina's fourteenth state park.

Andy Griffith Borrowed the Name for his New Show

Chances are if you grew up in the Appalachian Mountains, you probably already knew this one, but it's still fun to tell!

On October 3, 1960, CBS aired the first of what would eventually grow to 249 episodes of "The Andy Griffith Show".

Starring legendary Hollywood actor Andy Griffith, a native of nearby Mount Airy, North Carolina, the show borrowed many characters and places of Griffith's childhood – with slight changes in the geographic names: Mount Airy became Mayberry and Pilot Mountain became Mount Pilot. Character Orville Hendricks, the butter and egg man, was said to live at Mount Pilot. In one episode of the show, Barney Fife refers to himself and Sheriff Andy Taylor as "the law west of Mount Pilot."

The North Carolina Girl JFK Wanted to Marry

Appalachian Magazine Staff

On Saturday, April 27, 1940, a crowd of people gathered at a historic Charlotte mansion that was once owned by energy baron Buck Duke, in order to witness the holy matrimony of Frances Ann Cannon and John Hersey.

Hersey was an aspiring journalist who would later earn a Pulitzer Prize and Cannon was the daughter of a prominent Carolina family who often opened their home, The Duke Mansion, known as "White Oaks", to special visitors to the Queen City.

Among the individuals seated in the audience that spring afternoon was a 22-year-old Harvard University senior known to the bride simply as "Jack"; however, the entire world would later call him President John F. Kennedy.

Photo: Frances Ann Cannon, Courtesy of the Duke Mansion

The decision to visit Charlotte, North Carolina's Duke Mansion, the residence of the bride was not an easy one for the ambitious son of an ambassador. Prior to the wedding, Kennedy wrote to a friend, "I would like to go, but I don't want to look like the tall slim figure who goes out and shoots himself in the greenhouse half-way

Photo: President John F. Kennedy, three years following Frances Cannon's wedding.

through the ceremony."

Geoffrey Perret, author of Jack: A Life Like No Other, had this to say about Kennedy's relationship with the young woman from Charlotte: "Frances Ann Cannon was... witty, outgoing and confident. Every American housewife or hotel manager who bought a Cannon towel was making a small contribution towards this young woman's inheritance."

"Even so, there was a problem — the Cannons of North Carolina were rock-solid Presbyterians. Joe and Rose did not like his taking a serious interest in her; the Cannons were equally unenthusiastic about their beautiful daughter getting involved with a Catholic. But Romeo took Juliet to Harvard football games, paraded her in front of his friends and eventually proposed marriage. She turned him down."According to Perret, Cannon came from a family so rich Kennedy never had to question the sincerity of her interest in him and the young President-to-be was so smitten with her that the idea of marriage proved irresistible.

It is not known where or with whom the young Jack Kennedy spent the night that evening following the wedding of the woman many regard as being his first true love.

What we do know, however, is that JFK never forgot the Carolina girl and retained her memory for the remainder of his days.

"He was in love with Frances Ann Cannon," writes Lesa Holstine, adding, "He proposed to her, but she refused because he was Irish, Catholic, and Joe Kennedy's son. She sent him a telegram when he left for Europe saying, 'Stay away from the hay, darling. (Jack would describe himself as having hay fever when he wasn't well.) Love you, darling. Frances Ann.' That telegram is in the Kennedy Library. That meant Kennedy kept that telegram for his whole life."

In the ensuing years, the property would see several changes in ownership and would undergo a series of restoration efforts aimed at restoring the mansion to the splendor seen during the Roaring Twenties.

Coming full circle, the mansion would eventually fall into the hands of The Lynwood Foundation (a non-profit organization dedicated to preserving and protecting the estate) and would be renamed The Duke Mansion, after one of its earliest and most prestigious owners.

Today, the mansion features 20 individually decorated luxurious guest rooms, six of which offer shared sleeping porches.

Setting a gold standard in Charlotte hospitality, the Inn lends itself to corporations and organizations needing professional meeting space, as well as brides wishing to get married on the same grounds a heartbroken JFK once attended the wedding of his sweetheart...

Texas Pete: Born in North Carolina, not Texas!

Appalachian Magazine Staff

Throughout most of my life, I have held a great affinity for hot sauce — specifically for the 12-ounce bottles of the bright red liquid known as "Texas Pete".

Though my wife has evolved into a great cook, in the early years of our marriage, I was fortunate enough to have discovered that Texas Pete makes otherwise unpalatable food actually taste good and good food taste great!

Today, you won't ever catch me eating eggs, hot dogs, steaks, pizzas, or even a baked potato without the incredibly awesome cayenne-pepper hot sauce.

Growing up in the mountains of Southwest Virginia, I always assumed two things about Texas Pete:

#1.) That it came from Texas... I imagine that I wasn't alone on this one!

#2.) "Texas Pete" is a household product known throughout the United States.

One evening, I arrived just outside of Erie, Pennsylvania, where I'd be staying for a few days in a hotel and as is my custom, I made a quick trip to the local grocery store for a week's worth of "bachelor food". Of course, at the top of my list was Texas Pete.

"Excuse me, mam, where is your Texas Pete?" I asked the lady working in the grocery store, to which she [trying not to "LOL" in my face] responded, "Texas Pete? Is that even a real product or are you just joking with me?"

An older worker who was passing by overheard our conversation, to which he interjected, "I know what it is, follow me sir..."

As we walked through the grocery store, I soon found myself standing in front of a giant freezer looking at "Texas Toast".

Long story short — he had no idea what I was talking about either and neither did anyone else in the store!

Indeed, being such a huge fan of Texas Pete, I have come to realize that there are a number of misconceptions concerning this product.

To understand the true story of Texas Pete, you'll have to take a trip back to the year 1929... Not to Texas, but to Winston-Salem, North Carolina.

According to the company, legend has it that, when Sam Garner and his three sons were trying to come up with a brand name for the spicy new sauce they had created, a marketing advisor suggested the product be named "Mexican Joe".

The marketer believed that "Mexican Joe" would connote the piquant flavor reminiscent of the favorite foods of our neighbors to the south.

Sam Garner was opposed to the marketer's suggestion, stating, "It's got to have an American name!" Sam suggested they move across the border to Texas, which also had a reputation for spicy cuisine. Then he glanced at son Harold, whose nickname was "Pete" and the Texas Pete cowboy was born. Movie cowboys were very popular in the 1930's, men like Tom Mix and Hopalong Cassidy, representing a sort of universal image of rugged independence and self-reliance, the perfect ideal for a family business trying to survive tough times.

In the years ahead, the brothers would incorporate their business following World War II into T.W. Garner Food Company, as it is known today.

Though the company and its many products continue to change, two things have remained unchanged — they still produce Texas Pete and they're doing it in North Carolina!

"The current factory, built in 1942 and added onto too many times to count, sits on the original Garner family home site in northwest Winston-Salem. And the legendary Texas Pete, proud of his cowboy heritage but also a proud North Carolinian, continues to thrive!"

Old Time
Mountain Religion

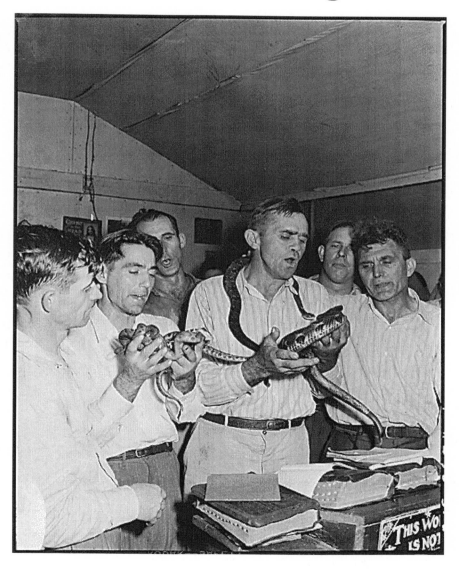

Footwashing at the Hardshell Baptist Church

Written by James Britton Cranfill in 1916

My father and mother were members of the Hardshell Baptist Church. It was made up of most excellent people. The Hardshell Baptists are very like the Missionary Baptists in their creed but differ somewhat in the interpretation of their creed.

On a certain Sunday, I went with my father and mother to the old time rawhide lumber church down on the south side of the Prairie. You may not know what rawhide lumber was, it was lumber sawed from oak trees. It was called rawhide lumber because it wouldn't stay put. It worked beautifully when green, but when the lumber dried under the heat of the summer sun it warped in every direction. This rawhide lumber warped in every conceivable fashion. For that reason, it had to be nailed very securely. If it were not thus nailed when green it never could be nailed because a nail can't be driven through a rawhide lumber plank after it seasons.

This church had a pine lumber floor and pine lumber seats many of which did not have any backs to them. On this particular Sunday Brother Abe Baker preached and then my father preached and Brother John Baker closed with an exhortation. These dear people would begin their services at about eleven o'clock in the morning and close them sometime in the afternoon, the time for the benediction varying with the number of preachers present and with the time it took for the Lord's Supper and the Foot Washing. After all three sermons had been duly preached and a closing hymn had been sung, Brother Baker came down out of the pulpit, opened his Bible and read the following verses from the 13th chapter of John: Now before the feast of the

"He riseth from supper, and laid aside his garments; and took a towel, and girded himself. After that he poureth water into a bason, and began to wash the disciples' feet, and to wipe them with the towel wherewith he was girded... Ye call me Master and Lord: and ye say well; for so I am. If I then, your Lord and Master, have washed your feet; ye also ought to wash one another's feet."

Preparation had been made by the deacons in anticipation of this exercise. The bread and wine had been procured as well as the basins and towels and water for the foot washers.

I reluctantly reveal a secret here. These dear good people when a foot washing time was approaching always very carefully washed their feet before they went to the foot washing. Not only that, but they put on the cleanest kind of clean hosiery. After Brother Baker had read the Scripture, I have quoted he laid aside his coat, girded himself with a towel, poured water into a basin and approaching Deacon Jack Bellamy, he knelt in front of him and said, "Brother Bellamy, may I wash your feet?"

Brother Bellamy assented and the dear man of God thus kneeling in front of Deacon Bellamy began to wash his feet.

Deacon Bellamy in the meantime had removed his shoes and stockings.

While this was going on the women of the church at the other end of the building were carrying on the same exercises. The men washed each other's feet and the women did likewise.

The greatest of decorum was preserved and the occasion was always a most solemn one. The foot washing began after the Lord's Supper was concluded. They first took the bread and wine just like other Christians do. This was done in great solemnity and then the foot washing followed.

After Brother Baker had washed Brother Bellamy's feet, Brother Bellamy, in turn, washed Brother Baker's feet. At the same time, my father was busy washing the feet of old Brother Asa Bellamy and he, in turn, washed my father's feet.

It was thus that going from one to the other and reciprocating this evidence of humility and love these dear people proceeded with their foot washing.

Many were the strangers who came down Hallmark's Prairie way to witness the foot washing exercises. But in every case as far as I can recall, those who came to scoff remained to pray.

There was nothing laughable in this solemn religious observance. Whatever else may be thought of it or said of it, it was true and will remain ever true that these simple folk believed profoundly that they were doing the will of God.

I must testify to be sincere that on every occasion when I was present at a foot washing, there was what the dear old folks would call "a splendid meeting."

They would when the exercises were concluded grasp each other's hand, shed tears of Christian joy, give voice to expressions of tenderest Christian love, and oft times these dear old soldiers of the Cross would be clasped in each other's arms.

Many were the misunderstandings and embryo feuds that would be settled on these foot washing occasions. No man could ever allow an enemy to kneel and wash his feet and no man could ever remain an enemy of the man whose feet he had washed. It was thus that whatever the meaning of the teaching of the Scriptures the ceremonial had its part in cementing the hearts of these dear people in the tenderest bonds of
Christian and neighborly affection.

Now and then as the exercises would close some of the sisters would shout aloud for joy.

A Glimpse Into the Snake Handling
Churches of Appalachia

Appalachian Magazine Staff

Photo: Snake handling service held in Lejunior, Harlan County, Kentucky at the Pentecostal Church of God, September 15, 1946. Company funds have not been used in this church and it is not on company property. Most of the members are coal miners and their families. (National Archives and Records Administration, photo by Russell Lee)

My mother was just a young girl when she first heard the thumping tambourines and squeals of mountain worship coming from "the bottom" near her West Virginia home.

"My mom and dad were 'again it', but soon curiosity got the best of my friend and me and it watn't long until the two of us had followed the mysterious sounds over the creek, through the thicket and to the bottom where the big white camp meetin' tent had been spiked into the ground."

The "mysterious sounds" she and her friend had heard was that of Appalachian religion and her vision was soon filled with dancing, screaming and beating of tambourines; an alien sight to my mother, who had been brought up in the more refined First Baptist Church.

"It seemed like total chaos, there was people everywhere. They were dancing, shouting, yelling and of course, holding snakes."

My mother's parents would eventually find out about her foray to a snake handling camp meeting and to hear her tell the story, her father was none too happy.

Though she never attended another "meetin' with snakes", the sights and sounds of that one night have never escaped her memory.

A handful of years later, the father of a classmate, who was a well known snake handling preacher in the area, died after having been bitten by a venomous serpent and as she recalled, the family did not mourn for him, stating, "Well he should'a had more faith and he wouldn't ah died."

Worship for West Virginia's snake handlers was much like so many other parts of life: difficult, dark and heavy in judgment.

But where does the uniquely Appalachian practice of snake-handling come from and why are folks still doing it?

To obtain this answer, we must first travel back in time to the closing days of Jesus' earthly ministry. Speaking to his apostles, Christ stated, "They shall take up serpents; and if they drink any deadly thing, it shall not hurt them; they shall lay hands on the sick, and they shall recover." (Mark 16.18).

For two millennia, the mainstream Christian interpretation of this verse was that Christ was speaking directly to his apostles, a church office that was to go extinct following the death of the last person to have seen Christ's physical earthly body. It was also believed that the Apostle Paul fulfilled this prophesy when he was ship wrecked, as recorded in the Book of Acts:

"And when Paul had gathered a bundle of sticks, and laid them on the fire, there came a viper out of the heat, and fastened on his hand. And when the barbarians saw the venomous beast hang on his hand, they said among themselves, No doubt this man is a murderer, whom, though he hath escaped the sea, yet vengeance suffereth not to live. And he shook off the beast into the fire, and felt no harm. Howbeit they looked when he should have swollen, or fallen down dead suddenly: but after they had looked a great while, and saw no harm come to him, they changed their minds, and said that he was a god." (Acts 28).

And thus the words of Christ concerning serpents were accepted as having been intended for the apostles only for the next 18 centuries throughout most of Christendom; however, all of this changed in the opening days of the 1900s in rural Appalachia.

Around the year 1910, a well known Church of God preacher named George Went Hensley of Grasshopper Valley in southeastern Tennessee, began preaching a literal interpretation of these verses and to prove their faith, he and his followers first began the practice of handling venomous snakes in the mountains of Appalachia.

In the following decade, the Church of God repudiated the practice of snake-handling, and Hensley and his followers formed their own body.

Around this same time period, serpent-handling in north Alabama and north Georgia originated with James Miller in Sand Mountain, Alabama. Miller apparently developed his belief independently of any knowledge of Hensley's ministry and Miller's teachings eventually became known as the Church of Lord Jesus with Signs Following.

Worship services usually include singing, praying, speaking in tongues and preaching. The front of the church, behind the pulpit, is the designated area for handling snakes. Rattlesnakes, cottonmouths, and copperheads (venomous snakes native to North America) are the most common, but even cobras have been used. During the service, believers may approach the front and pick up the snakes, usually raising them into the air and sometimes allowing the snakes to crawl on their bodies. The snakes are considered incarnations of demons, and handling the snakes demonstrates one's power over them. Members are not required to handle the snakes. Some believers will also engage in drinking poison (most commonly strychnine) at this time.

Over sixty cases of death as the result of snakebites in religious worship services have been documented in the United States. If a handler is bitten, it is generally interpreted as a lack of faith or failure to follow the leadership of the Holy Spirit. Bitten believers usually do not seek medical help, but look to God for their healing. George Went Hensley died in Florida in 1955 from a venomous snakebite.

Believers generally adhere to strict dress codes such as uncut hair, no cosmetics, the wearing of ankle-length dresses with pantyhose for women, and short hair and long-sleeved shirts for men. Most ministers preach against any use of all types of tobacco and alcohol.

According to ABC News, an estimated 125 churches practice serpent handling in the United States, most of which are concentrated in rural Appalachia, although some are as far away as Canada.

All Appalachian states except West Virginia outlawed the snake-handling ritual when it first emerged. West Virginia's state constitution does not allow any law to impede upon nor promote a religious practice.

Most snake handling, therefore, takes place in the homes of worshipers, which circumvents the process of attempting to obtain a government permit for the practice. Law enforcement usually ignores it unless and until they are specifically called in, which does not usually happen unless a death has resulted.

Snake handling was made a felony punishable by death under Georgia law in 1941, following the death of a seven-year-old of a rattlesnake bite. However, the punishment was so severe that juries would refuse to convict, and the law was repealed in 1968. The American Civil Liberties Union has defended the religious freedom of snake handlers against various attempts to have the practice banned.

A West Virginian's Vision to
Place Crosses Across America
Appalachian Magazine Staff

From as early as I can remember, three large crosses have stood on the north side of Interstate 81, alone in a cow pasture, just a few minutes east of Fort Chiswell, Virginia.

As a child, I always appreciated seeing these magnificent and larger than life crosses, though at the time, I cannot say that I fully understood the meaning of that most Holy symbol, nor did I realize the sheer effort required to plant those consecrated reminders across the nation.

The story of America's roadside crosses, the ones that have the two white crosses on the outside with a single yellow cross in the middle, begins humbly enough on January 27, 1925, in Craigsville, West Virginia.

On this date, a young child named Bernard Coffindaffer was born.

Raised by his father and stepmother, the young West Virginian would join the military at the age of sixteen.

Serving in the United States Marine Corps during the turbulent years of World War II, Coffindaffer provided for the defense of his nation for a period of six years; seeing active duty in the Pacific Theater, fighting at the bloody battle for the island of Iwo Jima, as well as serving in the occupation force at Nagasaki, Japan, following the end of hostilities.

Following his military service, the Marine returned to the Mountain State and worked in the years that followed, eventually earning a degree an associate degree from what was then Morris Harvey College (now University of Charleston.

Now a college graduate, the young entrepreneur found work in the oil industry, serving as a salesperson for a Charleston-based company.

In the years that followed, Coffindaffer would create a side business that specialized in washing coal. This proved to be lucrative and garnered the West Virginia native what some have described as a "small fortune."

Married, with four children, the Craigsville native's life would take an abrupt turn at the age of forty-two, when the World War II veteran knelt and softly asked Jesus to become his personal Saviour. Though he had heard the story of the cross thousands of times throughout his life, this time something seemed different. Something seemed real about the cross and the wealthy industrialist soon developed a true passion for the cross of Calvary.

In the days ahead, Coffindaffer's concerns would wane from increasing profits to reaching souls with the message of the cross.

Soon, the Appalachian resident had professed to friends and family that he had been called to serve as a preacher to forgotten Appalachian churches – ministering at seven different small churches in Pocahontas County, West Virginia.

After two heart by-pass operations, Coffindaffer liquidated his business and two years later had what he called a "genuine, marvelous, glorious vision," stating, "The Holy Spirit instructed, blessed, and dealt with me and told me how to go about installing these crosses. It was an experience you have once in a lifetime."

The following decades were spent gathering manpower, materials and resources to plant crosses alongside major highways all across America.

The first clusters of crosses were planted in September 1984 and in the years ahead more than 2,000 crosses were installed in the United States, Zambia and the Philippines.

According to family members, the crosses were "wooden, fashioned from telephone poles" and originally blue and gold.

In his final decade of life, Coffindaffer exhausted his earned wealth, spending more than $3-million on the project.

In a 1991 interview, the minister announced, "The crosses are to remind people to remember that Jesus was crucified on a cross at Calvary for our sins, and He will soon return."

Sadly, the project came to an abrupt end on October 8, 1993, as the 68-year-old suffered a heart attack at this home in Craigsville.

More than 21 years have passed since Coffindaffer has laid eyes on any of his crosses, which at the time of his death had been planted in 29 states.

Today, the vast majority of the Christian symbols he scattered across the nation are broken down and in disrepair.

One woman, Sara Stevenson Abraham, has stepped in to continue the West Virginian's work. She has formed a non-profit organization entitled Crosses Across America, Inc., headquartered in Vicksburg, Mississippi. The group is dedicated to locating the standing clusters of crosses and "getting them straightened, repaired, and restored." Abraham presents the story of the crosses for churches, civic organizations, television, and radio programs.

STUDY: More Expensive the Ring & Wedding, the Shorter the Marriage

Appalachian Magazine Staff

A study published by two Emory University economics professors isn't exactly music to the ears of jewelry retailers and wedding planners, but it sounds right in line with the mountain wisdom granny freely shared with all engaged couples — "it ain't the wedding, it's the marriage you need to be focused on."

In the study, the professors evaluated the association between wedding spending and marriage duration using data from a survey of over 3,000 ever-married persons in the United States.

"Controlling for a number of demographic and relationship characteristics, we find evidence that marriage duration is inversely associated with spending on the engagement ring and wedding ceremony," stated professors Andrew M. Francis and Hugo M. Mialon.

In 2013, the average wedding cost had grown to $29,858 and over the past seventy years, the wedding industry has grown substantially in part due to the rise of consumerism and industry efforts to commodify love and romance.

In 1959, Bride's Magazine recommended that couples set aside 2 months to prepare for their wedding and published a checklist with 22 tasks for them to complete. By the 1990s, the magazine recommended 12 months of wedding preparation and published a checklist with 44 tasks to complete.

"Spending between $2,000 and $4,000 on an engagement ring is associated with a 1.3 times greater hazard of divorce as compared to spending between $500 and $2,000," stated the study.

The study also found that spending $1,000 or less on the wedding is significantly associated with a decrease in the hazard of divorce in the sample of all persons and spending $20,000 or more on the wedding is associated with an increase in the hazard of divorce.

"In particular, as compared with spending between $5,000 and $10,000 on the wedding, spending less than $1,000 is associated with half the hazard of divorce in the sample of men, and spending $20,000 or more is associated with 1.6 times the hazard of divorce in the sample of women."

In their concluding thoughts, the professors wrote, "The wedding industry has consistently sought to link wedding spending with long-lasting marriages. This paper is the first to examine this relationship statistically. We find that marriage duration is either not associated or inversely associated with spending on the engagement ring and wedding ceremony."

What We Lost When We Lost Our Hymnals

Written by Tim Challies & Appalachian Magazine Staff

Few memories are as synonymous with church in my mind, as the sight of my mother holding up a raggedy old red hymnal and singing to the top of her lungs the songs of Zion.

Sadly, the number of children who are privileged to such memories in today's world is dwindling with each passing hour; partly because church is becoming an afterthought to so many and partly because many religious establishments are "moving past" the golden era of hymnals.

The following is an article written by Tim Challies, in which he seeks to remind church folk what they lose when they give up their hymnals:

If we were to go back in time twenty or thirty years, we would find that most churches had hymnals. They had hymnals because it was the best way of providing each member of the congregation with a copy of the songs. You'd hear it in every church: "Take out your hymnal and turn to hymn 154…" And then hymnals went the way of the dodo and we began to look instead to words projected on a screen. Here is some of what we lost along the way.

We lost an established body of songs.

Hymnals communicated that a church had an established collection of songs. This, in turn, communicated that its songs were vetted carefully and added to its repertoire only after careful consideration. After all, great songs are not written every day and their worth is proven only over time. Therefore, new hymns would be chosen carefully and added to new editions of the hymnal only occasionally. Churches would update their hymnals, and, therefore, their established body of songs, only once every ten or fifteen years.

We lost a deep knowledge of our songs.

When we removed the hymnal, we gained the ability to add new songs to our repertoire whenever we encounter one we deem worthy. And we do—we add new songs all the time. As we add new songs with greater regularity, we sing old songs with less frequency. This reduces our familiarity with our songs so that today we have far fewer of them fixed in our minds and hearts. Few congregations could sing even the greatest hymns without that PowerPoint screen.

We lost the ability to do harmonies.

Hymnody grew up at a time when instrumentation took a back seat to the voice. Hymns were most often written so they could be sung a cappella or with minimal instrumentation. For that reason, hymnals almost

94

invariably included the music for both melody and harmonies and congregations learned to sing the parts. The loss of the hymnal and the associated rise of the worship band has reduced our ability to harmonize and, in that way, to sing to the fullest of our abilities.

It often seems like all we want from the congregation is their enthusiasm.

We lost the ability to sing skillfully.

As congregations have lost their knowledge of their songs, they have lost the ability to sing them well. We tend to compensate for our poorly-sung songs by cranking up the volume of the musical accompaniment. The loss of the voice has given rise to the gain of the amplifier. This leads to our music being dominated by a few instrumentalists and perhaps a pair of miced-up vocalists while the larger congregation plays only a meager role. In fact, it often seems like all we want from the congregation is their enthusiasm.

We lost the ability to have the songs in our homes.

Hymnals usually lived at the church, resting from Monday to Saturday in the little pockets on the back of the pews. But people also bought their own and took them home so the family could have that established body of songs there as well. Families would often sing together as part of their family worship. It is easy to imagine a family singing "It Is Well With My Soul" after eating dinner together, but almost impossible to imagine them singing, "Oceans."

It is probably too late to go back to the hymnal. I am not at all convinced we ought to. But it is still worth considering what we lost along the way and how congregational singing has been utterly transformed by what may appear to have been a simple and practical switch in the media. That little change from book to screen changed nearly everything.

B&B's, Trees & Peas:
Traveling Appalachia

Romance, History & Charm:
Our Trip to Charlotte's Duke Mansion
Appalachian Magazine Staff

Photo: The Duke Mansion, Charlotte, North Carolina,
courtesy The Lynnwood Foundation

With impending snow and frigid temperatures looming in the forecast for Southern West Virginia, Allison and I made the decision to mark the ninth year of our marriage by heading south. Not too far into Dixie, but just enough to escape the abominable reach of icy road conditions and single-digit wind chills.

Our chosen target: Charlotte, North Carolina.

The straight shot provided by Interstate-77 puts the Queen City barely two hours from the West Virginia Stateline, but thanks to a history dating back to 1755, Charlotte is a distinctly southern community that carries the unique charm of a 21st century "New South" city.

By the time we crossed Lake Norman we had shed our heavy coats and roughly a half hour later, we were just yards from Bank of America Stadium, home of the Carolina Panthers.

According to the GPS on the dash of my vehicle, we were only 2 miles from our destination, The Duke Mansion.

"I can't believe we're only a couple miles from a secluded estate," whispered Allison, as we drove under the shadows of Charlotte's Center

City skyscrapers.

As we continued driving through one of the city's most historic neighborhoods, I couldn't help but notice the unusual layout of many of the streets. I would later learn that this is the result of the fact that a century ago, Charlotte experimented heavily with trolley cars and later converted their tram lines into streets for automobiles.

In a matter of seconds, the towering buildings of uptown Charlotte had given way to large hardwood trees and historic mansions.

At last, we had arrived.

Driving up the steep entrance that leads to the Duke Mansion, we passed a massive tulip poplar on the corner of the property; the 300-year-old tree is a rarity in its neck of the woods, as most of this section of Charlotte had been cleared and served as cotton fields during the 1800s.

As we approached the front entrance to the 102-year-old house, we were greeted by a large water fountain. And there it was: The ornate "H"-shaped, 2 1/2-story Colonial Revival style mansion I had been anxious to see all week.

Immediately, I couldn't help but notice the opulence of this upscale inn. Optional valet parking, attentive professional staff, and the home property itself, all gave testimony to its grandeur

Moments later, we had checked in at the front desk and were walking alongside a friendly staff member to our second story guest room.

No swipe cards here, guests to this historic mansion use old fashioned metal keys to access their room — this is a nice touch, as it adds to the feeling of being in a Roaring Twenties mansion.

Opening the door to the Nesbit Room (#207), we were greeted by a long hallway that led to our bedroom. To the right was a luxurious bathroom.

Walking into the bedroom for the first time, I was immediately impressed with the height of the ceiling, which reminded us of the inescapable fact that we were staying in a mansion that had previously served as the home to many of the South's most prominent individuals... As a matter of fact, a heartbroken John F. Kennedy once attended the wedding of a girl many historians claim was his first love at this very estate, a quarter-century before becoming President.

Just beyond the draped French doors was the sleeping porch which overlooked the garden and fountain down below.

The following day, Allison and I enjoyed a cup of coffee in the hanging swing of the shared porch in the quietness of the morning — blissed to the reality that only a mile away was Charlotte's busy I-277.

Unfortunately, it was still winter and our morning coffee on the back porch was cut short — we vowed to return in a handful of months and sip sweet tea while we watched a southern sunset.

Photo: Nisbett Room, The Duke Mansion. Appalachian Magazine.

As we enjoyed our breakfast and then strolled through the grounds of the historic estate, I couldn't help but appreciate how the mansion was so easily accessible and yet cosmos away from the world only a mile to our north.

Each room in The Duke Mansion is individually decorated. Ours featured a letter desk which reinforced the emotion of having stepped back in time into the world of the 19th-century industrial barons.

Another incredible observation made while spending a night at the mansion was the level of pride each member of the staff brought to work. It was clear that the high caliber employees place great attention to detail and service – going out of their ways to open doors for guests, providing service with a smile and exceptional facilities are all standard fare.

When the weather is warm, guests to the mansion can enjoy a 3-minute walk through the Myers Park neighborhood to several chic restaurants and shopping venues, including the Manor Theatre – a classic theater that first opened in 1947.

In addition to Panera Bread, Ben & Jerrys, and Starbucks, that are all within walking distance, other stores and eateries include Fenwicks Restaurant, Ginbu 401 and Stagioni.

On the way back home, Allison and I discussed the many things we love about Charlotte — a forward-looking city with endless miles of greenways, things to do and a vibrant atmosphere; yet equally impressive is that at its core, Charlotte is still a friendly southern town that hasn't forsaken its roots.

Here's to Charlotte and the desire to get back to one of its greatest gems as soon as possible!

Photos: TOP — View of the front of the mansion; Bottom — Sleeping Porch. Appalachian Magazine

Rails to Trails:
Virginia's New River Trail State Park
Appalachian Magazine Staff

Compared to the rest of the Commonwealth, the area known by locals as Southwest Virginia is a unique region compared to other parts of the Old Dominion. Far from the hustle and bustle of the nation's capital city and even farther from the tidewaters of the Chesapeake Bay, the forgotten land of Virginia's panhandle is hardly recognizable as even being in the same state as places such as Fairfax, Norfolk and Richmond.

Here, roughly 60 miles southwest of Roanoke, cows outnumber people and the most common reason for a traffic jam on local roads is a sputtering tractor transporting rolls of hay from one field to another. Life is slower, more relaxed and yes, the people are even a tad bit friendlier here than in other parts of Virginia... Okay, a lot more friendly.

Today, the region's economy has become well balanced between agriculture and industrial

Photo: New River Trail,
Courtesy Virginia State Parks

manufacturing, but a century ago, the mining of various minerals, particularly iron ore, served as one of the staples of the local economy in the counties of Pulaski, Wythe, Grayson and Carroll.

With small communities all along the Upper New River being rich in minerals needed to power the Industrial Revolution, surveyors from Norfolk & Western Railroad set out in 1882 to find a suitable route for a spur linking the main line in Pulaski to Mount Airy, North Carolina. At the time, the Pulaski area was known as Martin's Station.

By 1887 nearly 29 miles of the route, originally known as the Cripple Creek Extension, had been completed, linking the community of Austinville to Pulaski and by 1904, the line had been extended all the way to Galax – linking the communities of Pulaski, Foster Falls, Austinville, Ivanhoe, Fries (pronounced "freeze") and Galax together.

According to Trail Link, "While iron ore was the primary source of freight, there was also other outbound traffic, including agricultural products, milk, forest products, less-than-carload movements (which could include anything an individual wished to ship but not did fill an entire freight car), and cotton mills in the Fries area. Notable inbound shipments included coal, animal feed, fertilizer, agricultural products, and oil. After the N&W fell into receivership during 1896, it seemed new management lost interest in completing the extension to Mt. Airy, perhaps because the railroad now already had two notable lines into the Tarheel State at Durham and Winston-Salem..."

The line typically had two trains that ran each day and Norfolk & Western continued to provide passenger service until after World War II, making its final run on September 5, 1951.

Not too many years ago, it wasn't that difficult to find an old timer around those parts who had ridden a passenger train into one of these communities for a day or two to visit relatives or attend school or something of the sort; sadly, first-hand stories such as these are quickly becoming a lost memory throughout this part of Appalachia.

The railroad continued to operate the line even into the mid-1980s, during the early Norfolk Southern (NS) years.

Unfortunately, with many lines customers closing, including New Jersey Zinc, Norfolk-Southern elected to abandon all remaining operations south of Pulaski, and trains made their last runs on October 5, 1985.

The following year, the Commonwealth of Virginia acquired the abandoned land as a donation from the Norfolk-Southern Corporation and attempted to do something exceptional: convert the former rail into a trail.

Volunteers worked feverishly, transforming the overgrown line into a linear "trail park", the first of its kind in Virginia, and in May 1987, The New River Trail State Park opened, with only 4 miles of trail available for use.

Three decades later, history has proven the advocates of the rails to trails program true visionaries as 57 miles of trails have been made available to hikers, walkers, bicyclists and horseback riders and the park has seen as many as 1.2 million visitors in a single year, pumping critical money into the rural community and allowing entire villages to spring up, catering to the needs of cyclists and trail users.

Photo: Jogger on the New River Trail State Park, Courtesy, Virginia State Parks.

Running north to south, trail mile markers begin at Dora Junction outside of Pulaski. The Town manages a spur trail that connects the park to the renovated train depot where visitor services, including a bicycle shop, are available. From Dora Junction, the trail travels through the railroad villages of Draper and Allisonia; past the 19th-century Jackson Ferry Shot Tower; through the historic mining towns of Austinville, Foster Falls, and Ivanhoe; and past the Buck and Byllesby hydroelectric dams to Fries Junction.

At this point, the trail splits, with one section branching off to follow Chestnut Creek to Galax and the other continuing along the New River to Fries. Bicycle shops and other visitor services are available in both Galax and Fries.

The New River Blueway runs south to north along with the river's current, and begins south of Boone, North Carolina and runs through New River Gorge to Fayetteville, West Virginia. Along the trail, boat access points with parking are available at seven different locations and primitive, canoe-in campgrounds are also located along the river at various spots.

Thirty years ago, the local Virginia communities along the New River received what seemed to have been devastating news — their railroads and mines were about to disappear. Rather than attempt to live in the past, however, they tried something that had never been done in the state before and a generation and a half later, their children are enjoying the fruits of their foresight.

Drive Through America's Bloodiest Tunnel

Appalachian Magazine Staff

Photo: Dingess Tunnel, Used by permission from Norfolk Western Collection

Hidden deep within the coal filled Appalachian Mountains of Southern West Virginia rests a forgotten land that is older than time itself. Its valleys are deep, its waters polluted and its terrain is as rough as the rugged men and women who have occupied these centuries old plats for thousands of years.

The region is known as "Bloody Mingo" and for decades the area has been regarded as one of the most murderous areas in all of American history.

The haunted mountains of this region have been the stage of blood baths too numerous to number, including those of the famed Hatfield's and McCoy's, Matewan Massacre and the Battle of Blair Mountain. Even the county's sheriff was murdered this past spring, while eating lunch in his vehicle.

Tucked away in a dark corner of this remote area is an even greater anomaly – a town, whose primary entrance is a deserted one lane train tunnel nearly 4/5 of a mile long.

The story of this town's unique entrance dates back nearly a century

Photo: Modern view of Dingess Tunnel, open to motorists, courtesy of Prosserman

and a half ago, back to an era when coal mining in West Virginia was first becoming profitable.

For generations, the people of what is now Mingo County, West Virginia, had lived quiet and peaceable lives, enjoying the fruits of the land, living secluded within the tall and unforgiving mountains surrounding them.

All of this changed, however, with the industrial revolution, as the demand for coal soared to record highs.

Soon outside capital began flowing into "Bloody Mingo" and within a decade railroads had linked the previously isolated communities of southern West Virginia to the outside world.

The most notorious of these new railways was Norfolk & Western's line between Lenore and Wayne County – a railroad that split through the hazardous and lawless region known as "Twelve Pole Creek."

At the heart of Twelve Pole Creek, railroad workers forged a 3,300 foot long railroad tunnel just south of the community of Dingess.

As new mines began to open, destitute families poured into Mingo County in search of labor in the coal mines. Among the population of workers were large numbers of African-Americans.

Despising outsiders, and particularly the thought of dark skinned people moving into what had long been viewed as a region exclusively all their own, residents of Dingess, West Virginia, are said to have hid along the hillsides just outside of the tunnel's entrance, shooting any dark skinned travelers riding aboard the train.

Though no official numbers were ever kept, a countless number of black workers are said to have been killed at the entrance and exits of this tunnel.

Norfolk & Western soon afterward abandonment the Twelve Pole line. Within months two forces of workmen began removing the tracks, ties, and accessory facilities.

Soon, silence soon reigned in the rugged mountains overlooking the area. Gone were the whistles of locomotives and the rumble of cars. Nothing but long, winding bed of cinders, a few decayed ties, several steel bridges remained.

For decades the skeletal remains of Norfolk & Western's failed railway line stood as a silent testimony to the region's ghostly ways.

In the early 1960's, however, the resourceful men of the mountains commandeered the former railroad line and built upon its beds a road for motorists to travel upon.

Unfortunately, residents of this impoverished region failed to secure funding from the state's legislature to improve the tunnel and bridges, thus today – over half a century later – residents of this community are forced to drive atop countless one lane train bridges and a nearly mile long one lane tunnel.

To the residents of this community, such a drive is just another part of their daily routine, however, for visitors unfamiliar with the thought of driving through a one lane tunnel with a fifty ton coal truck at the other end, such an experience can be a rush, to say the least.

One writer said the following of his experience driving through the Dingess Tunnel:

"Locals state that proper usage is to turn lights on, indicating that you are entering the tunnel. Drivers from the other end know not to enter if lights are on. We saw an 18 wheeler tanker go through while there, but it is a tight fit. Water drips from the top and one can barely see as it takes a while for eyes to adjust. Locals state that the roadway was dirt up until a couple of years ago and had deep holes in it. Now it is paved, but no lighting."

How Virginia's "Lover's Leap" Got Its Name

Appalachian Magazine Staff

This past spring, we briefly said goodbye to the mountains of Appalachia and pointed our car east toward the historic Martinsville Motor Speedway in Virginia's southside region. With the NASCAR touring series scheduled to kick-off the month of April with competition in the Old Dominion, we game for the opportunity to watch some of the hottest and intense racing on the circuit.

Traveling along US Route 58 from western Virginia to Martinsville provided us with a course that showcased a part of Virginia that has largely remained unchanged for the better part of a century — a silent time capsule of a forgotten way of life in the mountains of Dixie.

Amid the picturesque farms, rolling hills, rickety country stores and the general feeling of "this is the one place in the world I'd love to move to tomorrow if I could", was an unexplainable peace and happiness that can only be achieved via the backroads of rural America.

Not long after passing through the Meadows of Dan, home of the iconic Mabry Mill, the two-lane J.E.B. Stuart Highway turned upward and soon we found ourselves climbing to an altitude of 3,000 feet.

To our south was the unmistakable knob of Pilot Mountain in nearby North Carolina.

As we reached the top, we came upon a roadside overlook with the familiar name of "Lover's Leap", offering a north facing vista toward the city of Roanoke, overlooking the headwaters of the Dan River..

According to the Virginia officials, the steep mountainside cliff owes its name to an Appalachian-style Romeo and Juliet love story.

"In the 1600's, the Indians inhabited the Blue Ridge Mountains. White settlers started arriving and began clearing land to farm. Conflict arose between the Indians and the settlers. Legend has it that the son of a settler saw the twinkle in the eyes of the Chief's daughter, Morning Flower, and was immediately love-struck. The couple began to meet secretly and their love continued to grow. The young man and Indian maiden were threatened and shunned. With the beautiful rock and wildflowers as their backdrop, they jumped into the wild blue yonder ensuring they would be together forever. As you gaze out at Lover's Leap, you can still see the evidence of their love in the beautiful view and hear them whisper in the cool evening breezes."

Admittedly, this story sounds like there may have been a few embellishments along the way, but one thing that cannot be exaggerated is the incredible beauty of this Patrick County, Virginia, overlook.

God's Thumbprint: Burke's Garden, Virginia

Appalachian Magazine Staff

Just a handful of miles from where Virginia's Blue Ridge spine meets the rounded off hills of West Virginia is a geographic oddity that has been described as "God's Thumbprint".

Located in the heart of Tazewell County, Virginia, Burke's Garden is an oval, bowl-like valley that is surrounded entirely by mountains and measures roughly 8.5 miles long by 4 miles wide.

At 3,000 feet in elevation, the site is the highest mountain valley in the Commonwealth of Virginia and serves as some of the most fertile farmland in the state thanks to the reality that water drains on all sides into the valley.

Though the land feature resembles a large volcanic crater from the air, it as actually created when massive underground limestone caverns collapsed and is believed to have once been the bed of an ancient sea.

According to Virginia Tourism, the site was first discovered in the 1740's by James Burke while hunting in the area. "The name 'Burke's Garden' was given to the valley as a joke in 1748 after Burke planted potato peelings by the campfire of a 1748 surveying party. The next year, a fine crop of potatoes was found."

The community was an outpost of German immigrants who settled in the back country frontier in the late 18th century.

Thanks to the circling mountains around the settlement, the area remained isolated for over a century, until agents from the Vanderbilt family discovered the property in the late-1800's.

Contacting local farmers in hopes of purchasing the land in order to build a large estate in the valley, the Vanderbilt's were disappointed when all landowners refused to sell.

Dejected, the Vanderbilt's went farther south to the hills of North Carolina and constructed the Biltmore Estate near Asheville.

In the 1990's, a small number of Amish families moved to Burke's Garden and have gradually begun building a thriving Amish community in the heart of Appalachia.

Today, lines of scooters can be seen daily outside the Burke's Garden School and Community Center where the Amish now have their own school. The General Store is owned by the Amish and visitors enjoy barbecue and sandwiches on thick slices of home baked bread. Visitors can buy baked goods and vegetables, bike on area roads, hike and hunt in nearby Jefferson National Forest.

The only vehicular entrance to Burke's Garden may be accessed approximately 25 miles west of the Rocky Gap, Virginia exit of Interstate 77 in Bland County, Virginia. The community can also be viewed from the Appalachian Trail.

US-52: America's Other Great Highway

Appalachian Magazine Staff

Over the past 75-years, much has been made about historic U.S. Route 66, often affectionately referred to as the Main Street of America.

Though the famous route linking Chicago to California has certainly earned its place in history, there is another route – just as old as Route 66 – that deserves just as much of the nation's admiration, it is U.S. Route 52, America's other great highway.

Beginning at the Charleston Harbor in sunny South Carolina, the 2,072 miles of the 89-year-old route run northwest all the way to the Saskatchewan / North Dakota border.

Like the hundreds of communities the one-lane (Portal, ND), two-lane (Calmar, IA), three-lane (Welch, WV), four-lane (Charleston, SC) and six-lane (Wytheville, VA) route passes through, the road itself is a pure representation of the unique stories, values and struggles of each of the eleven states the roadway links together.

In South Carolina, the route begins on Charleston's Broad Street, passing underneath Palmetto trees and picturesque southern mansions.

The 150-miles of U.S. Route 52 in North Carolina link the coastal plains to the Appalachian Mountains, passing by the fascinating ancient pinnacle known as Pilot Mountain. The Saura Indians, the region's earliest known inhabitants, called the mountain "Jomeokee", meaning "great guide". Just a handful of miles down the road, the route cuts north and becomes the Andy Griffith Parkway, passing through Mount Airy, the hometown of Andy Griffith and inspiration for the fictional community known as Mayberry.

Crossing into the Commonwealth of Virginia, the route's elevation climbs from 1,296 ft. at the stateline to nearly 3,000 ft. in just 8.5 miles, atop Fancy Gap Mountain — a notorious stretch of U.S. 52 so feared by early southbound truckers that the route and mountain inspired J.R. Williams to write a well known ballad, "Rolling Down Fancy Gap."

Continuing through Virginia, the route passes by Wythe County's Historic Jackson's Ferry Shot Tower, a 1700s- era tower used to construct lead bullets. Briefly joining with Interstates 81 and 77 for a nine-mile stretch in Wytheville, the route breaks from the six lanes and again takes the winding trail up Big Walker Mountain, passing by the 100-ft. high observation tower known as the Big Walker Lookout, offering visitors a view of the surrounding countryside some 3,586 ft. above sea level.

Caution to the would be traveler of U.S. 52 (WV) who is quick to become carsick, the route's winding path through the Mountain State's southern coalfields is certain to have you pulled over by the road long before you reach the top of Horsepen Mountain! Also, lookout for coal trucks, ATVs (which are legal to drive on this historic highway in many West Virginia communities thanks to the Hatfield McCoy ATV trails), speed traps and left-right-left-left-right-left-right turns... If you've ever driven on what is known as the National Coal Heritage Highway (US-52 in West Virginia) you know exactly what we're talking about!

It is West Virginia's version US-52 that highlights the Appalachian region's great struggle just to survive over the past half century, especially in McDowell County, the American County that is literally going extinct. At the same time, however, US-52 also showcases the Mountaineer spirit of persistence, as transportation officials are in the process of upgrading the route to a high-speed four-lane divided highway, a route that will cut the driving time from Williamson, West Virginia, to Bluefield, West Virginia, from +120 minutes to 87 minutes.

Between the West Virginia cities of Williamson and Huntington, the route briefly crosses into Kentucky twice, thanks to the impenetrable West Virginia mountains. Word of caution to the traveler along this stretch: the speed limit in West Virginia is 65 mph, but drops to 55 mph along the Kentucky portions.

Crossing the Ohio River via the Nick Joe Rahall II Bridge, the route winds along the banks of the Ohio River, the largest tributary, by volume, of the Mississippi River.

Through the Buckeye State, the route passes through the Ohio localities of Portsmouth and Cincinnati, passing directly in front of the Cincinnati Bengal's 65,000-seat Paul Brown Stadium, before heading northwest into Indiana.

The route through Indiana enjoys a less prominent role than in other states, serving as a secondary-bypass between Indianapolis and LaFayette before entering the Land of Lincoln, Illinois.

It is in Illinois that the route zigzags through the nation's heartland, passing just yards from the Chicagoland Speedway near Joliet, as it intersects the historic pathway of Route 66.

Continuing west, Route 52 crosses the Mississippi River near Savanna, Illinois, though the river as this location more closely resembles a swampy lake.

In Iowa, the great highway runs north along the western banks of the Mississippi River, passing through the heart of Dubuque, a charming midwestern town whose brick streets date back to 1833.

A far cry from the mountain highway of the two Virginias, Route 52 enters the plains of Southern Minnesota in big sky country, where cornfields, silos and flatlands abound for a countless number of miles.

Eventually, the route's agricultural views giveway to the urban skyline of Minneapolis.

Dissecting St. Paul, the route passes by casinos and the farmers markets of both St. Paul and Minneapolis, passing by the campus of the University of Minnesota, before cutting north back toward the rural heartland of America's upper Midwest. In total, the U.S. route runs 377 miles through the Land of 10,000 Lakes, before crossing its final border at the Red River of the North and entering Fargo, North Dakota.

From Fargo, the route continues west for about 75 miles, before turning northwest toward the Badlands of North Dakota.

The remainder of the route doesn't link any major American cities, instead, it merely connects little towns with funny names – cutting through the center of places such as Foxholm, Anamoose, Bowbells, and my personal favorite, Lignite!

The American highway reaches its final town in Portal, North Dakota, where it meets the Canadian Border Patrol and Saskatchewan Highway 39, an undivided 271-mile long highway connecting North Portal and Moose Jaw.

It is impossible to define the culture of US-52, as encompasses eleven separate states and covers more than 2,000 miles. To put it simply, the road highlights our nation's greatest accomplishments and vistas, as well as our greatest struggles. If you're traveling US-52, you can expect to see real America… and all of America! This is why we believe that US Route 52 is America's Other Great Highway!

The Incredible Story of the Blue Ridge Parkway

Appalachian Magazine Staff

This past fall, the *Appalachian Magazine Travel Bloggers* headed east, spending some much needed family time in the Blue Ridge Mountains of Old Virginia.

Our journey began in the Central Virginia community of Madison Heights, a suburb of Lynchburg, nestled along the banks of the James River at the foot of the Appalachian Mountains.

Heading north on State Route 130, we soon intersected the Blue Ridge Parkway near Otter Creek, approximately midway between the cities of Lexington and Lynchburg.

Dating back to the mid-1930s, the Department of Interior's Blue Ridge Parkway traces its origins to the administration of President Franklin D. Roosevelt and was originally christened "the Appalachian Scenic Highway."

Though September 11th will forever be remembered as one of the darkest days in American history, it was on this storied date in 1935 that work began on one of the greatest treasures in all of Americana – a 469-mile long path that would serve as a vehicular natural history museum, art gallery and Appalachian safari for nearly 13-million visitors each year.

Unlike Interstates 77 and 81, which flank the Parkway, this two-lane byway is not designed to get motorists to a destination, but is instead the ultimate destination – and for good reason, check out these incredible pictures we took in a single afternoon!

One of the interesting stories in the history of the Parkway is unlike so many other public works, construction on the Blue Ridge Parkway did not cease during World War II. Instead, the CCC crews were replaced by conscientious objectors to serving in the world war.

In the end, construction of the Parkway took over 52 years to complete, with the final stretch around North Carolina's Grandfather Mountain opening in 1987.

Today, the scenic byway continues an additional 109 miles past its proposed ending point in Central Virginia on the Shenandoah National Park's Skyline Drive.

On this October afternoon, however, our family wasn't concerned about the history of the incredible and scenic roadway, we just enjoyed taking a break from the interstate, taking a break from tractor-and-trailers and bumper-to-bumper traffic. To put it simply, we just enjoyed riding in a low stress environment where the maximum speed was 40 mph, ugly metal guardrails were replaced by natural rocks and gas station billboards were exchanged for 200-mile vistas of distant mountains.

"This is so cool dad," exclaimed my daughter, as she leaped across

Otter Creek on large millstones that date back generations.

A handful of minutes later, the two of us were posing for a picture atop what she described as "the biggest rock ever!"

Some thirty minutes later and no more than 3,500 feet down the road, our entire family was bravely walking the Harry Flood Byrd Memorial Bridge.

Described by visitors as "one of the highlights" of this part of the Parkway, the 1,040-foot vehicular bridge also doubles as a pedestrian walkway across the historic James River, leading to a piece of West Virginia history some 45-miles away from the nearest West Virginia county, a fully restored canal lock of the nineteenth century James—Kanawha Canal.

Originally surveyed by George Washington, the canal was intended to link the east flowing James River, which discharges into the Chesapeake Bay, to the northwestern flowing New / Kanawha River, which travels in the opposite direction, ultimately releasing into the Gulf of Mexico, via the Ohio and Mississippi Rivers.

In a prophetic statement looking almost a century into the future, Washington worried whether Virginia – as was originally mapped – would be able to remain united, stating, "people's faces are naturally turned in the direction of the flow of their rivers," pointing out that eastern Virginians and their counterparts beyond the Blue Ridge were literally facing in different directions.

The canal was birthed by the Virginia legislature in an effort to create an eastern passage to the ocean for what would eventually become Southern West Virginia.

In the end, the formidable mountains of Appalachia proved too costly and impenetrable for the plan to succeed and the canal's construction was halted in the Virginia town of Buchanan, only 63-miles from the New River.

If only the unforgiving terrain of western Virginia had been a little more cooperative, if only the Richmond legislature had placed just a little more emphasis upon seeing the project completed – if only. Perhaps there would be no West Virginia, perhaps there would have been no Civil War, perhaps American history would have forever been altered. If only.

At the risk of sounding like an incredible nerd, coming face to face with this 160-year-old restored canal was one of my personal highlights of the trip – just realizing the purpose behind its construction and understanding the implications of its failure.IMG_4558

Other highlights of the afternoon drive included the warm and colorful fall foliage and the opportunity to meet so many incredible people, who just like us, enjoyed taking a break from the interstate – choosing to spend the day capturing panoramic views and making memories as opposed to… anything and everything else!

Museum Dedicated to "Housecats" Opens in North Carolina

Appalachian Magazine Staff

Attention all cat lovers out there… this article is just for you! You may want to amend this year's summer plans to include a trip to the high mountains of western North Carolina community of Sylva, where the American Museum of the House Cat is now open.

The museum opened on April Fools Day of this year, but when it comes to the 10,000 housecat artifacts included inside the facility, there's absolutely nothing to joke about — this is one serious collection.

According to the museum's website, the collection includes: Fine 'picture art' going back to the late 1800's, modern and folk art, rare cat advertisements, vintage and antique toy cats (many of which are automations from the 1890's), and vintage advertising, ranging from clocks to storefront and window display items.

"There is not another private collection of this magnitude and value in America," stated museum officials.

The museum was been opened to help support the Catman2 Cat Shelter, the first no-kill animal shelter in Jackson County, North Carolina, and the first cats only, cat shelter in western Carolina to reject the practice of keeping sheltered cats in cages instead of allowing them to roam free in large open spaces.

"The premise to an open or group shelter, came from my belief that no cat commits a crime by: being a stray, being abandoned by its owner, finding itself in a cat carrier on my doorstep, or coming to my shelter by any other means. Therefore, if no crime had been committed, why should that cat be locked in a cage like a criminal? I have operated Catman2 with this presupposition for the past sixteen years with a more than I expected level of success," stated Harold Sims Founder and President of Catman-2 Inc. a not-for-profit, cats only shelter serving its WNC community since 1996.

"I have been collecting cat related items for the past thirty years or more and have amassed a large collection of high quality cat related items. I want to share the collection in a way that will entertain and educate the public about the wonders of the House Cat and its interrelationship with man," stated Sims.

"It is said that there are 25 million cat lovers in America and there is only one other cat museum in the United States, in the town of Alliance [in] northeast Ohio. Cat lovers love cats, and will visit a museum opened in their honor."

Organizers of the museum say there is room for the museum to grow and their hope is for "The Museum of the House Cat" to become a major attraction in western North Carolina, with proceeds going to help support cat shelters and attracting additional tourism to the region.

Individuals wishing to learn more about the House Cat Museum of America may do so by visiting the official website of the museum or by calling the museum: 828-421-0275 or 828-506-1236. The museum is located at 4704 Highway 441 South, Sylva, North Carolina, NC 28779

Kentucky's Natural Bridges (Yes, plural!)

Appalachian Magazine Staff

The Commonwealth of Virginia may boast of having a "natural bridge" once owned by Thomas Jefferson, but the Commonwealth of Kentucky can boast of having more than a dozen naturally occurring bridges!

Natural Bridge of Kentucky

The Bluegrass State's most famous geological arch is found in the Daniel Boone National Forest, east of Lexington. There, the sandstone "Natural Bridge of Kentucky" rises some 65 ft. over the mountainside, spanning nearly 80 ft. across.

This Kentucky gem became one of the Commonwealth's four original state parks in 1926.

In addition to the natural bridge, which hikers can actually walk around atop... or for that matter allow their feet to dangle over the edge (which we would strongly discourage!), the Natural Bridge State Resort Park is also home to several other unique sandstone rock formations, including the Balanced Rock (a huge block of sandstone balanced on the edge of a cliff near the Natural Bridge).

In the early days of the Park, it was called the Sphinx because, when viewed from the correct angle, it crudely resembles the Sphinx in Egypt. Although it is now called the Balanced Rock, it is in fact a pedestal rock – a single piece of stone that has weathered in such a fashion that its midsection is narrower than its cap or its base. This formation is one of the biggest and most perfectly formed examples of a pedestal rock east of the Rocky Mountains

The 2,250 acre park offers more than 20 miles of hiking trails; however, a sky lift provides a convenient access point to the natural bridge for individuals unwilling to spend the entire day hiking.

Creelsboro Natural Bridge

Another Kentucky natural arch may be found in Russell County's Creelsboro Natural Bridge, also known as Rockhouse.

Located approximately 7 miles downstream from Lake Cumberland's Wolf Creek Dam, the Rockhouse has a span of 104 ft., making it one of the largest natural bridges in the nation.

First discovered in 1770 by a group of hunters, Rockhouse was designated a National Natural Landmark by the U.S. National Park Service in 1987.

Koger Arch

Koger Arch, a 54 ft. wide, 18 feet high and 91 feet across arch just south of Whitley City. This arch is slightly harder to reach than the others, but well worth journey.

Carter Caves State Resort Park

With over 30 miles of hiking trails, Carter Caves State Resort park presents the hiker with seven natural bridges throughout the park. The Cascade Trail is a three-quarter mile trail passing through Box Canyon. The Three Bridges Trail winds three and a quarter miles and includes the park's largest natural bridge, the Smokey Bridge, which stands an impressive 90 feet (27 m) high and 120 feet (37 m) wide. This trail also passes by Fern Bridge and Raven Bridge as it meanders through the park. The half-mile Natural Bridge Trail passes beneath a third natural bridge, the only one in Kentucky that is paved and supports traffic.

The bottom line is this – Virginia may have a natural bridge, but Kentucky has several natural bridges!

Appalachian Living, Food & Gardening

PAW PAW: America's Forgotten Fruit

Appalachian Magazine Staff

It's difficult to even begin to comprehend the amount of mountain knowledge that has been lost over the past half-century in the hills of Appalachia — so many of the basic skills for simply surviving have vanished with the dying off of our region's old timers and many fear we have lost basic skill sets that will take generations to re-learn.

Today, very few people living in the mountains of Appalachia even know how to identify sassafras, let alone make it into a tea. Same thing goes for a dozen other effective home remedies that are now ancient history, tucked away in some dusty book one seldom reads.

One of the greatest losses of mountain knowledge over the past generation is, in my opinion, how our country simply forgot about what was once upon a time its favorite fruit tree: The Paw Paw.

The largest edible fruit to grow in the United States, the paw paw was often referred to as "the poor man's banana" and is native to 26 different states.

As described by horticulturist Barbara Damrosch, the fruit of the pawpaw "looks a bit like mango, but with pale yellow, custardy, spoonable flesh and black, easy-to-remove seeds."

Pawpaw fruits have a sweet, custardish flavor somewhat similar to banana, mango, and cantaloupe.

Nineteenth-century American agronomist E. Lewis Sturtevant described pawpaws as "... a natural custard, too luscious for the relish of most people..."

Ohio botanist William B. Werthner noted that "the fruit ... has a tangy wild-wood flavor peculiarly its own. It is sweet, yet rather cloying to the taste and a wee bit puckery – only a boy can eat more than one at a time."

Despite their "puckery" nature, the fruit became a staple part of the diet of early Appalachian settlers.

In 1541, Spanish explorers found Native Americans cultivating the fruits along streams and rivers east of the Mississippi.

The Iroquois used the mashed fruit to make small cakes that were dried and stored. The dried cakes were soaked in water

and cooked to make a sauce or relish that was served with corn bread. Raw and cooked fruits were dried by the sun or on a fire. These were stored for use in the future or taken on hunts.

The Cherokee used the inner bark to make cordage. By twisting the bark, they made string and strong ropes.

The Lewis and Clark Expedition consumed pawpaws during their travels, particularly while traveling via the nation's rivers.

Chilled pawpaw fruit was a favorite dessert of George Washington, and Thomas Jefferson planted it at Monticello, his home in Virginia.

Unfortunately, due to the fact that Paw Paws cannot be mass-produced and profitably shipped by commercial fruit entities, their consumption has all but ended in the age of consumerism; Paw Paws can only be kept 2–3 days at room temperature, or about a week if refrigerated. The easily bruised pawpaw fruits do not ship well unless frozen.

As kayaking and a host of other river activities are coming back into the mainstream, Americans are slowly rediscovering the fruit tree that never went away… we just forgot about it as a people.

Why Your Grandparents Would "Plant by the Signs"

Appalachian Magazine Staff

I can hear her shaky voice like it was yesterday, "You need to get your taters in the ground tomorrow, 'cause the signs is right'."

The last "Granny Woman" of our family, my 'Mamaw' served as a wealth of knowledge for most everything we encountered in our West Virginia community, and in the springtime, folks from all over the holler would seek her advice regarding when to plant their gardens. She was a firm believer in "planting by the signs".

Described as devilish by some and extolled by others; I never truly understood what any of it meant until long after she was gone, but as I age, I find myself becoming more and more fascinated by the complex astrological system she relied upon for the better part of a century.

Today, most everyone who plants a garden does so as a mere hobby or at the very most in an effort to supplement their grocery store purchases; however, 150 years ago, a successful garden was often the difference between surviving the winter and starving to death.

As a result, the folks "back in the day" took a far more serious approach to planting and the moon's phases helped to serve as a guide to improve their chances of a successful garden.

"And God said, Let there be lights in the firmament of the heaven to divide the day from the night; and let them be for signs, and for seasons, and for days, and years... And God made two great lights; the greater light to rule the day, and the lesser light to rule the night: he made the stars also." — Genesis 1.14, 16

In its simplest of forms, "planting by the signs" means that you plant crops that will produce their fruits above the ground during the waxing moon (the time between a new moon and a full moon — when the moon is getting bigger), while plants that produce their crop below the ground must be planted during a waning moon (the time between a full moon and a new moon — when the moon is shrinking).

Lori Elliott, writes, "Many old-time farmers also planted and harvested by the astrological signs. Barren signs, such as Aquarius, Gemini, and Leo, would have been considered ideal times for plowing and cultivating the soil, while fertile signs such as Cancer, Scorpio, and Pisces would have been considered the best times for planting seeds."

Old timers lived by these signs for centuries, but the one question remains: is there any science to back up their traditions? And that's the million dollar question!

25 years ago, the New York Times set out to determine if planting by

the full moon was a bright idea or lunacy; unfortunately, they were not able to reach any definitive conclusion.

Scientists at NASA stated that planting by the moon was pure "mythology" and nothing more; however, Dr. Mac Cathey Ph.D. in plant physiology, told the Times that his grandmother gardened by the signs in North Carolina. "And she was a tremendous gardener... But all our high-germinating seeds and pesticides have damped out our ability to read the signs... It's like music. We can't sight-read anymore."

Regardless of whether you're a believer or not, chances are the folks in your family tree religiously planted by the signs only a few generations ago.

How to Make Natural Orange Cleaner
Kim Holloway Stalcup

Photo courtesy: Appalachian Mountain Roots

Appalachia has always been the land of self sufficiency. Whether it's the coalfields of West Virginia or the Smokies of Carolina, the people who call these mountains home have been forced to get by with what they had — even when what they had wasn't much.

Kim Holloway Stalcup, an 8th generation resident of Cherokee County, North Carolina, runs the blog Appalachian Mountain Roots, where she shares the history, recipes and traditions of the mountains she calls home.

Stalcup recently wrote the following:

"The isolation that comes with mountain living didn't give residents any choice. It was do or die. The only way people got around in early

Appalachia was by foot or horse and wagon. The roads were steep and narrow but even if they could have gotten to town easily and often, there was little money to be spent for the things they needed. When a family did have money, it was spent on necessities that they couldn't find or make such as coffee, sugar, lamp oil, and shoes."

With this thought in mind, the Appalachian blogger wishes to share the following recipe for an all natural (and effective) cleaner, made from orange peelings.

"I recently bought some organic oranges & instead of throwing away the peels, I laid them aside to dry. Once I had enough to fill a quart size Ball jar, I poured white vinegar over them, screwed on the lid, & put it in a cool dark place. After around 2 weeks, I drain some of the new orange cleaner into a clean spray bottle at a 3:1 ratio of vinegar to water. That's it...I now have a naturally anti-bacterial cleaner that is also non-toxic & very frugal. Vinegar can be used on its own but I'm not a fan of the smell. The orange peels add a nicer aroma to the cleaner. You can also use the peels from lemons and limes!"

Pretty awesome huh?

Why Mountain People Would
Cook a Coin in Cabbage Each New Year
Appalachian Magazine Staff

Photo Courtesy: Tereberna

My city-slicker grandmother who did not grow up in the mountains of West Virginia, recalled with a twinkle in her eye, the first time she had new year's dinner with my grandfather's family in the coalfields of Southern West Virginia.

"I remember sitting down and they brought out a big pot of cooked cabbage and each person had a cabbage roll plopped down onto their plate... About five minutes into dinner, I took a bite and it felt like I had put something metal into my mouth.

"Trying my best to retain the lady-like charm I thought I possessed, I quietly excused myself from the table and soon found what appeared to be a dime spit into my napkin..."

Though at first she was baffled as to how a dime had found its way into her dinner, she soon underwent her first of many lessons in Appalachia 101.

In the years ahead, she would come to embrace the mountain tradition of eating cabbage on the first day of the year, though she never completely bought into the idea of hiding a silver coin in one of the rolls for good luck to the unsuspecting individual who found it!

"Why not eat cabbage on the first day of the year," she once quipped, "all the stores in West Virginia have it on sale the day before New Years."

But where did this seemingly bizarre mountain tradition come from and what does it signify?

Turns out, like so many other aspects of Appalachian tradition and culture, this New Year's practice was born more out of necessity than convenience.

With many mountain families growing the vast majority of the food they consumed all the way up to a generation ago, by mid-winter, cabbage was often the staple vegetable.

Keeping considerably longer through the cold months than most other veggies and being significantly cheaper made this the ideal New Year's food for a large family.

Over the course of time, this unassuming custom would grow into a tradition in the mountains.

In the years ahead, the Scots-Irish who settled large portions of Appalachia (or kept it from being settled!) married the dinner with an old-world custom of hiding various coins in cooking mashed potatoes with kale or cabbage on special occasions and holidays – the recipient of which would be blessed in the year ahead.

Another new year tradition observed throughout the mountains was one known as "First Footer".

This belief taught that if the first person to set foot in your house after the New Year was a tall and dark haired man, you have good luck for the coming year.

Times have always been tough for the people of Appalachia and they often have found themselves running low on hope — which is why the mountain people have so resolutely clung to a countless number of traditions and superstitions; especially when it comes to the new year... which reveals that they've always been looking forward.

It is important to note that this tradition requires a pure silver coin, not a clad coin as most are today.

These old traditions have become a major part of our region's heritage and must be shared before they are forgotten altogether. We wish you and your family a blessed new year... whatever tradition you may observe!

Dandelions: The Plant That Was Never Supposed to Have Been in America

Appalachian Magazine Staff

If time travel were somehow possible and the average American had the opportunity to step back in time 500 years, he or she would encounter a North American continent that would appear almost alien from the place they know as home today.

Towering trees 50 feet around dotted the virgin forests of the nation's East, blanketing a landscape that closely resembled an unexplored jungle. Roaming cougars silently stalked their prey for days in the dark mountains of Appalachia, letting out their hellish cries each night.

Put perhaps what the time traveler would find most incredible about the old "New World" would be what wasn't here a half-millennia ago: There were no apple trees, no pigs and not a single horse on the continent — each of these items were imported from Europe.

Most notably, however, there wasn't a single dandelion to be found from Canada to South America.

Dandelions have for countless millennia served as a staple plant throughout Europe and Asia, with even the Ancient Egyptians using them for medicinal purposes. And for good reason. According to the Maine Organic Farmers and Gardeners Association, "Dandelions are more nutritious than most of the vegetables in your garden. They were named after lions because their lion-toothed leaves healed so many ailments, great and small: baldness, dandruff, toothache, sores, fevers, rotting gums, weakness, lethargy and depression. Not until the twentieth century was the underlying cause of many of these symptoms realized: vitamin deficiencies... They have more vitamin A than spinach, more vitamin C than tomatoes, and are a powerhouse of iron, calcium and potassium."

In Midevial England, the yellow flowers were celebrated both as a decorative yard flower as well as a source of medicine.

Unfortunately for colonists to the New World, the strange land they encountered was void of this terrific plant.

In an effort to have a reminder of home, dandelion seeds were quickly brought to America and planted throughout New England.

However "Once out of the bottle... the genie proved uncontrollable," writes Nature North.

Having no natural predator, the invasive species thrived in the new world, moving westward at a dizzying pace, reaching the Pacific Coast centuries before the same land was ever settled by the descendants of the individuals who first introduced the plant to the New World.

In no time at all, several generations of dandelion seeds had been windswept throughout the colonies and within only a few short decades, dandelions were growing throughout the continent.

As settlers moved west, they were greeted by a European immigrant that had reached the unsettled lands west of the Mississippi long before their arrival — the dandelion.

Embracing the plant, American settlers used the dandelion to make wine and dye, season salads, and even to serve as a coffee substitute when baked and ground.

Today, the dandelion is one of the few plants found in all 50 states and are even encouraged in pastures, acting as an important source of food for cattle and sheep.

So the next time you're ready to tackle that innocent smiling child who is on the brink of scattering dozens of those lighter than air seeds with one sharp exhale of their lungs, just keep in mind that long before you were ever born, or even many of your ancestors were born dandelions had subdued the entire continent and the descendants of the Mayflower have been in an unwinnable quest to rid the land of this once celebrated flower.

Pokeweed:
America's Tasty Salad and Highly Poisonous Plant
Appalachian Magazine Staff

Photo: Mature Phytolacca americana (Pokeweed) in a field in Macomb County. These plants are to be avoided long before they reach this maturity.

I'm sure that for the unsuspecting outsider the sight of my 110-lb granny climbing a West Virginia hillside with a burlap sack tied around her shoulder would have proven to be quite a spectacle – especially when she'd hunch over and begin filling her bag with what would appear to the untrained eye as nothing more than a bunch of weeds.

If asked what she was planning to do with all those "weeds", I have no doubt that this 5ft.-nothing tower of a woman would have replied with something akin to, "these here ain't no weeds – this is my poke salad."

As a child, I can't remember how many times I enjoyed a "second heap'n" of granny's poke salad – little did I know at the time, I was actually eating one of the more poisonous plants in all of Appalachia!

Naturist Jonathan Schechter warns, "Don't be fooled by the deep purple berries and munch a sample. All parts of this plant are poisonous to mammals... Herbalists tend to agree that when properly prepared the very small tender spring shoots can be consumed–but if you make an error your reward can be as simple as cramping, vomiting and diarrhea or can be dangerous heart rhythms, coma and death."

Despite the fact that pokeweed can be found throughout most of the Continental United States, the people who call the Appalachians and Dixie home are the folks who have really taken a liking to this plant – considering its leaves a delicacy.

Foodie Larry Rankin writes, "It is a poisonous weed, related to night shade, but if prepared for consumption correctly, it is actually considered a delicacy by many Southerners. In fact, in its cooked form, the pokeweed is so popular that many southern states hold yearly festivals in the early spring to commemorate it."

According to Rankin, the cooked version of this weed is properly referred to as poke sallet, but I doubt that my granny would agree! The word sallet traces back to Middle English and refers to a mess of greens cooked until tender.

Though all parts of the plant are toxic and pose risks to human and mammals, the highest concentrations of poison is found in the rootstock, then in leaves and stems and then in the ripe fruit. The plant generally gets more toxic with maturity, with the exception of the berries (which have significant toxicity even while green).

Researchers at the Ohio Agricultural Research & Development Center found that "Children are most frequently poisoned by eating raw berries. Infants are especially sensitive and have died from eating only a few raw berries. Adults have been poisoned, sometimes fatally, by eating improperly prepared leaves and shoots, especially if part of the root is harvested with the shoot, and by mistaking the root for an edible tuber. Research with humans has also shown that common pokeweed can cause mutations (possibly leading to cancer) and birth defects. Since the juice of pokeweed can be absorbed through the skin, contact of plant parts with bare skin should be avoided."

So how in the world did such a violent weed find its way onto my family's mountain table? Who knows! Perhaps desperate times call for desperate measures!

Turns out, pokeweed has been poisoning mountain folk for centuries – especially from ingestion of berries and roots that were mistaken for parsnip, Jerusalem artichoke, or horseradish.

Still, Poke has persisted as a beloved springtime mountain food for generations.

According to old timers, the young leaves can be eaten prior to chambered pith formation but must be cooked – boiled three times in fresh water each time. It is also important that the purple skin is peeled away. Traditionally, poke leaves are with fatback and cooked some more to add flavor.

Appalachian Magazine strongly discourages its readers from preparing pokeweed unless they truly know how to do so and are confident in their ability and knowledge. No part of this article is intended to serve as a recipe or "how to" guide in preparing pokeweed but is offered merely as a cultural and historic documentation.

The bottom line is this: As tasty as it may be, at the end of the day, you are still eating a highly toxic plant!

Cornbread & Milk: Fine Appalachian Dining

Written by Kim Holloway Stalcup

Earlier this week, I made a big pot of deer chili and a cake of cornbread to go with it. The chili was good but I only had one thing on my mind when I pulled that sizzlin' skillet from the oven – I was going to get to enjoy a big glass of cornbread and milk for a snack that evening. It is so good and can be a meal all by itself. In fact, I've enjoyed it for a meal countless times. You know those days when you're just a little hungry but a sandwich just ain't going to cut it? A glass full of crumbled up, warm cornbread with sweet milk poured over it…yeah, that'll hit the spot. This is something that has been enjoyed in Appalachia for generations.

My Granny and Pa are the ones who introduced me to this delicious tradition. They usually used sweet milk (regular whole milk) but also enjoyed buttermilk. I've never been able to drink buttermilk so I always use sweet milk.

In Ronni Lundy's incredible cookbook, Victuals: An Appalachian Recipes, she says:

"Give us this day our daily cornbread…" could be the standard grace for tables all around the mountain South." She is absolutely right. It is a regular item on the table throughout southern Appalachia. I'm so glad, aren't you?!

Growing up, we ate cornbread with just about every meal. I never thought much about it until I went away to college. We had spaghetti in the cafeteria and I mentioned that I would like to have some cornbread to go with it. You would have thought that I had grown a second head! My college friends quickly informed me that my bread preference should be garlic bread not cornbread. Like I said, we ate cornbread with just about everything, including spaghetti. They didn't know how good of a thing they were missing.

This article was written by Kim Holloway Stalcup, who is the 8th generation to call Cherokee County, NC home. Her love of Appalachia led her to start the blog, Appalachian Mountain Roots, where she shares her love of Appalachian history, communities, food, crafts, traditions…her roots.

Why Some People Cut Their Hair Based Upon the Moon's Phases

Appalachian Magazine Staff

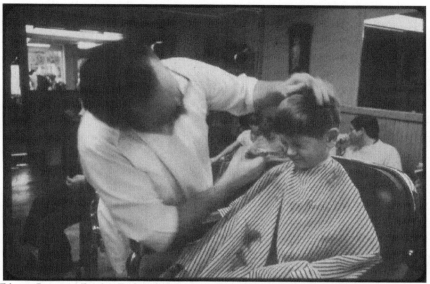

Photo Courtesy: Parks, Deborah, Photographer (NARA record: 8467939)

The folks of Appalachia have always been a superstitious lot — I can't recall how many times I've seen my father refuse to close a pocket knife someone else had opened or how many people I have watched family members go out of their way to ensure they left a building through the same door they had entered.

This past year, Appalachian Magazine published an online article entitled, "Why Your Grandparents Planted by the Signs" (also included in this section of the print publication), something I never truly understood as a child, but a reality to which I was keenly aware — we wouldn't be able to plant certain crops until granny would tell us "the signs was right."

One reader offered a very simple explanation as to the "why", when he simply replied, "Because it works!"

To my astonishment, however, we received hundreds of comments and messages from individuals whose families took these beliefs to a level far past my own — relying upon "the signs" to do everything from getting a haircut to determining when to potty train a child.

The basis many people use to serve as a foundation for the belief that the phases of the moon can have a direct effect upon one's plants, their hair and children's bodies comes from the opening words of Genesis:

"And God said, Let there be lights in the firmament of the heaven to divide the day from the night; and let them be for signs, and for seasons, and for days, and years… And God made two great lights; the greater light to rule the day, and the lesser light to rule the night: he made the stars also."
— Genesis 1.14, 16

"G'ma and Dad always [relied upon the signs]! Oh yes, it works! For the pottytraining and weaning from bottle, also for cutting hair at right date to make it grew slower/faster. Our God made our bodies and the earth to be in sync…" wrote one reader.

If you're thinking that cutting one's hair based upon the phases moon is some archaic relic of Appalachian mountain lore, you might be shocked to learn that the writers at Glamour explored this topic a few years after one of the individuals serving in their "Girls in the Beauty Department" was thumbing through a Farmers' Almanac and came upon a lists for the "best dates for cutting hair to increase growth, right alongside its suggested dates for planting crops or mowing the lawn."

Sandi Duncan, managing editor for Farmers Almanac kindly explained to fashion writer Petra Guglielmetti the back story behind such a belief:

"Many people believe that the moon has a direct pull not only on the tides, but a variety of other living things on earth."

Including hair.

Schwarzkopf International, a worldwide brand that offers tips for the care of one's hair, had this to say:

"Conditions during the waxing moon promote hair growth after a haircut. Therefore, you should cut your hair between the new and full moon if you want your hair to grow fast after a haircut. If you wear short hair and you want your hair to grow as slowly as possible you should cut your hair during the waning phase of the moon (between the full and new moon). Your short hairstyle will keep its shape longer."

But the begging question remains: Is all of this talk superstition or science? Is "lunar haircutting" just plain lunacy or is there something to it? I'm not sure, but I intend to begin taking notes regarding my hair over the next few months!

Born in Southwest Virginia: "Mountain Dew"
Appalachian Magazine Staff

Long before the soda craze of the early-1900s, the term "Mountain Dew" had been used to describe a leading beverage among the mountain people of the Appalachians – albeit a far less, shall we say, "legal drink".

In fact, a popular Irish folk song dating back to 1882 exclaimed:

> *Now learned men as use the pen*
> *Have writ' the praises high*
> *Of the rare poteen from Ireland green*
> *Distilled from wheat and rye*
> *Away with your pills, it'll cure all ills*
> *So take off your coat and grease your throat*
> *With a bucket of mountain dew.*

But today, we're going to talk about the history of the other "Mountain Dew" — the one that comes in a green can and is generally seen on the edges of picnic tables at backyard barbecues throughout "Dew Country."

Obtaining its name from the generic mountain word used to describe "whiskey", it should come as no surprise to learn that Mountain Dew was first developed as a mixer-drink for bars in the Knoxville, Tennessee, area in 1940.

The original formula was invented by Tennessee beverage bottlers Barney and Ally Hartman.

According to an article first published in the Virginia Pilot roughly 23 years ago, former Marion Mayor Marshall E. Guy said the drink "never took off" while the Harman's controlled the brand.

The duo first approached Coca-Cola, asking for a partnership to help them get their struggling drink to on the right track, but the soft drink giant turned down the offer.

Ultimately, the pair sold the rights to their formula and brand to the Tip Corporation of Marion, Virginia.

Bill Jones of the Tip Corporation immediately went to work attempting to make the brand marketable and eventually developed an entirely new drink in the process.

"'He fixed it so it had just a little more tang to it,' Guy recalls. 'He'd take little cups marked A, B, C, and D around to high-schools and drug stores and factories and ask people which of the mixtures in them tasted best. That's how he developed his formula.'" reported Larry Maddry.

Jones' new recipe, which was launched in 1961, called for extremely higher levels of citrus flavoring and caffeine — a combination that found a receptive audience in the taste buds of the local townspeople of Marion, Virginia.

Mountain Dew quickly grew in popularity throughout Southwest Virginia and in August 1964, Jones traveled to New York City and sold his newly developed brand to Pepsi.

As the story goes, he returned to his small Virginia town where he was greeted by his friends, opened up his wallet and stated, "Well fellas, I'm $20 short of being a millionaire."

A hat was then passed around and soon, Jones had obtained the $20 needed in order to officially be a millionaire!

With the soft drink manufacturer Pepsi now controlling the Mountain Dew brand, distribution was ramped up and soon folks from Florida to Canada were enjoying the heavy-sugar, heavy-caffeinated concoction.

Today, even in the face of numerous detracting media stories, the vast majority of which focus on the health effects excessing drinking of Mountain Dew can have upon a person, Mountain Dew enjoys an unshakeable position at the top of its league: MtnDew accounts for 80-percent of citrus soft drinks sold within the U.S., while Coca-Cola Company's Mello Yello, Surge, and Dr Pepper Snapple Group's Sun Drop must split the difference.

The next time you "Do the Dew," you can thank Marion, Virginia, resident William "Bill" Jones.

How Pigs got to America:
The Story of Wild Boar & Bacon

Appalachian Magazine Staff

There are few things more synonymous with the Appalachian lifestyle as a good ole hog. We eat it for breakfast each morning and those of us who were fortunate enough to have enjoyed a true mountain upbringing can still smell the indescribable stench that permeated from the massive barrel of boiling water each November. With over 1 billion pigs alive on the planet at any given moment, the outlook for this species is one of the best of all creatures roaming the seven continents — and this nation is no exception.

One of my earliest memories has me standing outside of a pigpen with my grandfather, throwing in whatever slop was being served up as swine dinner for the day.

To put it simply, throughout my life, pigs have been about as American as apple pie!

Interestingly, like just about everything else on this continent, hogs, boars, pigs, (or whatever other word you use to describe these animals), are non-native to this hemisphere and were introduced to the New World by European settlers and explorers. The first pig to have stepped foot upon our nation's soil was probably only a few steps behind the first white person to have ever done so.

Turns out, the history of pigs is a far more interesting subject than perhaps one would have ever imagined!

Dating back thousands of years before Christ, the Chinese were the first to have domesticated swine and by the time of Jesus' nativity, pigs had become a staple of diet throughout the Roman Empire; except in and around Jerusalem, where the Jews' religion forbade the eating of pork — this law was based upon "a belief that pigs were unclean since they ate waste, and there was the fear of disease (no doubt associated with contracting trichinosis from eating improperly cooked pork..." writes Mick Vann.

However, the demand for swine received a major boost around the year 40AD when the Apostle Peter, a Jewish Christian, experienced the following vision from God, which revealed that it was now acceptable for God's people to eat pig:

"Peter went up upon the housetop to pray about the sixth hour: And he became very hungry, and would have eaten: but while they made ready, he fell into a trance, And saw heaven opened, and a certain vessel descending upon him, as it had been a great sheet knit at the four corners, and let down to the earth: Wherein

were all manner of fourfooted beasts of the earth, and wild beasts, and creeping things, and fowls of the air. And there came a voice to him, Rise, Peter; kill, and eat. But Peter said, Not so, Lord; for I have never eaten any thing that is common or unclean. And the voice spake unto him again the second time, What God hath cleansed, that call not thou common." — Acts 10

In the centuries ahead, the teachings of Islam would ban the eating of pigs, as would most Jews, but in Christian Europe, the teachings of Acts 10 would pave the way for the consumption of pork to not only flourish but to expand around the world.

The short time to maturity, large reproduction numbers and the fact that they would eat just about anything that was unfit for human consumption all worked to secure the swine's place in Western Civilization as a meat of choice among the populace.

With the dawning of the age of exploration, explorers also came to appreciate the pig, as traveling with cattle onboard a cramped ship was completely out of the question. The pig, on the other hand, proved to be more than an accommodating traveler — helping to convert unwanted trash into food along the journey and providing meat for the weary upon making landfall.

Pigs were first introduced in the 1500's to what is now the southeastern U.S. by Spanish Explorer, Hernando DeSoto.

Kept as pets, the piglets and pigs faithfully followed explorers, breeding along the way and scouring the virgin forests for food. When the need arose, the explorers would kill one of the pigs, prepare it as food and continue on their journey… with the other pigs in tow.

Due to the thick vegetation, difficult landscape and stubborn nature of the animals, not all pigs stayed with the search parties and it was not uncommon for pigs to be separated from the group. Other pigs would be intentionally left in an area of rich food, with the explorers planning to return and hunt the animals when food became scarce.

In the years that followed, these "lost pigs" grew into a sizable feral population with very few predators to stop them.

This proved as both a blessing and a curse to Americans on the western frontier, as the wild animals were available for food if one could successfully hunt it, but on the flipside, gardens and fields could quickly become destroyed by the animals.

Eventually, many of these wild pigs were either domesticated or extinguished and in the years ahead, razorbacks ceased being the nuisance they once were to farmers in the Southeast.

In the late-1800s wealthy landowners began restocking their properties with wild boar and in no time at all, the animals had escaped and were intermixing with already established feral pig populations throughout the nation

"The most successful boar introduction in the US took place in western North Carolina in 1912, when 13 boars of undetermined European origin were released into two fenced enclosures in a game preserve in Hooper Bald, Graham County. Most of the specimens remained in the preserve for the next decade, until a large-scale hunt caused the remaining animals to break through their confines and escape. Some of the boars migrated to Tennessee, where they intermixed with both free ranging and feral pigs in the area. In 1924, a dozen Hooper Bald wild pigs were shipped to California and released in a property between Carmel Valley and the Los Padres National Forest. These hybrid boar were later used as breeding stock on various private and public lands throughout the state, as well as in other states like Florida, Georgia, South Carolina, West Virginia and Mississippi."

In recent years, wild pig populations have been reported in 44 states within the US, most of which are likely wild boar-feral hog hybrids. Pure wild boar populations may still be present, but are extremely localized.

The traditional diets of the American South and Appalachia are heavy in pork, whether it's bacon, chitlins, BBQ or pig feet… and it's all thanks to European explorers and their pet food. So that's the history of how boar and bacon came to be in America!

Opossums: Once a Celebrated All-American Meal

Appalachian Magazine Staff

Only a handful of generations ago, there were few things as valuable in the mountains and back hollers as a good possum dog. A canine that could tree America's only marsupial often meant the difference between a family going hungry for the evening and one eating high on the, eh hum, possum. Foreign to any animal known to Europe, the early settlers at Jamestown found the American Opossum to be one of the most intriguing features of the new world.

In 1608, famed explorer John Smith wrote about the nocturnal animal, stating, "An Opassom hath an head like a Swine, and a taile like a Rat, and is of the bignes of a Cat. Under her belly she hath a bagge, wherein she lodgeth, carrieth, and sucketh her young."

In the days ahead, Virginia's early settlers soon allowed their fascination for opossums to be turned into an appetite for the animal that is about the size of a domestic cat.

In the 1856 book, "Audubon," a typical fall day in early America was described, a day that ended climatically with the harvesting an opossum:

"On a bright autumnal day when the abundant rice crop has yielded to the sickle and the maize has just been gathered in when one or two slight white frosts have tinged the fields and woods with a yellowish hue ripened the persimmon and caused the acorns, chesnuts and chinquepins to rattle down from the trees and strewed them over the ground, we hear arrangements entered into for the hunt. The opossums have been living on the delicacies of the season and are now in fine order and some are found excessively fat – a double enjoyment is anticipated: the fun of catching and the pleasure of eating this excellent substitute for roast pig"

In an era when food was scarce and few enjoyed the opportunity to partake of pork, possums served as a critical fill-in.

Even as recently as 1962, the Joy of Cooking published an article regarding how to properly prepare a possum, stating, "If possible, trap 'possum and feed it on milk and cereals for 10 days before killling. Clean, but do not skin. Treat as for pig by immersing the unskinned animal in water just below the boiling point. Test frequently by plucking the hair. When it slips out readily, remove the possum from the water and scrape. While scraping repeatedly, pour cool water over the surface of the animal. Remove small red glands in small of back and under each foreleg between the shoulder and rib. Parboil, page 134, 1 hour. Roast as for pork, serve with turnip greens."

Other possum recipes included baking the animal into a pie or pastry… sounds yummy!

Though you'll be hard pressed to find someone who will readily admit to eating opossums in 2017, the animal's role upon the North American continent has not diminished by measure — infact, they are possibly more important to our nation today than ever before: Rarely transmitting diseases to humans and being surprisingly resistant to rabies — mainly because they have lower body temperatures than most placental mammals — opossums limit the spread of Lyme disease by eating ticks.

Yes, they're ugly and you may find yourself playing possum if you ever find one on your dinner plate, but make no mistake about it, the North American Opossum is one of the most valuable critters your eyes will come in contact with all year!

Golden Delicious Apple:
First Discovered by Chance in W.Va.

Appalachian Magazine Staff

There are few things as refreshing as a sweet tasting apple, and there are few apples that are as sweet to the taste as the Golden Delicious — which is why this apple is the sixth most sold variety in the entire nation according to the US Apple Association. This statistic is really impressive when you consider the fact that approximately 31 billion apples are harvested each year.

Despite its popularity, the Golden Delicious is actually a newcomer to the block — in fact, just about every American apple is an emigrant.

When European colonists first arrived in the new world they were disappointed to discover that their newfound continent did not contain any edible apples; the only apple trees in America were crab apples.

Soon, seeds from Europe were soon being planted throughout the colonies and in the years ahead, American settlers would begin to perfect the art of grafting — merging two separate plants in order to create a new type.

Among the nation's founders, Thomas Jefferson was fascinated by the science of grafting apples and experimented with several apple varieties at his Monticello plantation.

In the century that followed, grafting apples would become a newfound hobby of civilizations of nearly every continent.

Rowan Jacobsen, author of Apples of Uncommon Character, says, "Every Granny Smith stems from the chance seedling spotted by Maria Ann Smith in her Australian compost pile in 1868."

At the turn of the 20th century, new apple trees were turning up across the nation and West Virginia was no exception.

On October 18, 1962, the Charleston Daily Mail published an interview with an 87-year-old man, J.M. Mullins, who claimed to know the real history of the Golden Delicious apple tree.

"The true story of that first Golden Delicious apple tree never has been told. But son, I'm here to tell it now, for the first time. There are a lot of facts about that tree that haven't been told before. Told straight, that is... What I'm telling you is fact. I was there."

"I was born in 1876 on the farm where that apple tree later became famous. My dad was L. L. Mullins, who owned the farm.

"Now one day, when I was about 15 years old, that would have been about 1891, dad sent me out with a big old mowin' scythe to mow the pasture field. I was swingin' away with the scythe when I came across a little apple tree that had grown about 20 inches tall. It was just a new little apple

144

tree that had volunteered there. There wasn't another apple tree right close by anywhere.

"I thought to myself, 'Now young feller, I'll just leave you there,' and that's what I did. I mowed around it and on other occasions I mowed around it again and again, and it grew into a nice lookin' little apple tree and eventually it was a big tree and bore apples. Now my dad later gave that piece of the farm in a trade to my brother, B. W. Mullins, and later still he traded the farm place to Uncle Anderson Mullins.

"Uncle Anderson had a brother-in-law named Gus Carnes, and one day Gus and Uncle Anderson decided to send some of the apples to the Star Brothers nursery to tell what kind of apple it was. And that was when the tree became famous and started the Golden Delicious apple line, for it was that tree that has produced every last one of the Golden Delicious apple trees that have ever grown anywhere."

In 2010, an Italian-led consortium announced they had decoded the complete genome of the Golden delicious apple. It had the highest number of genes (57,000) of any plant genome studied to date.

On February 20, 1995, the Golden Delicious was designated the official state fruit of West Virginia by a Senate resolution and in 2013 the United States Postal Service issued a set of four 33¢ stamps commemorating apples, including the 'Golden Delicious'.

West Virginia is the originator of many vegetable and fruit crops, including the apples Grimes Golden, and the Guyandotte, which is believed extinct.

Tall Tales and
Mountain Legends

Did the Irish Make it to Appalachia Before Columbus "Discovered" America?

Appalachian Magazine Staff

Each October, the entire nation celebrates the life of Christopher Columbus, crediting him for "discovering" America in 1492 – but if you're like me, you find this concept somewhat laughable in and of itself, as millions of people were already living on the continent for thousands of years before Columbus was even conceived; however, we'll save that debate for some other day!

Instead, today, we're going to explore the unimaginable and incredible scenario in which Columbus' voyage to the Caribbean was predated by nearly a thousand years by Christian Irish missionaries, who not only landed on America's mainland but explored as far inland as Mingo County, West Virginia.

Though the evidence is hardly enough to put someone to death over, the mounting case does deserve more of a credible look than many are allowing.

Archaeologists first began exploring the possibility of ancient Irish missionaries in the new world, roughly a generation ago, after local residents discovered ancient markings and engravings on large boulders near a strip mi community of Dingess.

PHOTO: Dingess Petroglyph Markings
Taken by Appalachian Magazine Staff

Discovered in the 1980s, the slabs of rock were found on property owned by the Marrowbone Development Corporation and immediately became the source of study for scholars from around the world, as the markings were said to resemble ancient Irish letters known as Celtic Ogham.

In October of 1988, representatives from the Irish Embassy, including the nation's secretary of cultural affairs met with archaeologist Robert Pyle to examine the ancient rock carvings, referred to as petroglyphs.

Speaking to members of the media, Pyle was quoted as having said, "They're really unique. They have Christian religious symbols that are identifiable, many of them identifiable were recorded very early... The markings appear to be from around as early as the eighth century to the 12th century A.D."

The veteran archaeologist said that he believed the markings were made by early Irish missionaries who followed major trails through the mountains, stating, "It's really a tremendous discovery."

Pyle is not alone in his belief that the Irish were roaming the hills along the Tug Valley centuries prior to Columbus' voyage.

Dr. Barry Fell, a biologist who has studied numerous archaeological sites and ancient languages, contended that ancient West Virginia Petroglyphs were indeed written in the ancient Irish language known as Ogham.

Translating rock markings found in neighboring Wyoming County, West Virginia, Dr. Fell concluded that the ancient message carved into the rocks read: "At the time of sunrise, a ray grazes the notch on the left side on Christmas Day, the first season of the year, the season of the blessed advent of the savior Lord Christ. Behold he is born of Mary, a woman."

The translation leads Fell to believe the ancient markings are part of an ancient solar calendar created to bear a Christian message.

An article that appeared on WyomingCountyHeritage.com states:

"To try and prove this theory a small group decided to verify the translation. Calculating the difference between the Julian calendar, used until the 16th Century, and today's Gregorian calendar, they met at the petroglyph just before sunrise on December 22, 1982. Quietly they waited as the sun climbed in the east, spilled over the mountains, and streamed its rays toward the cliff face before them. They watched in amazement as the first shaft of sunlight funneled like a flashlight beam through a 3-sided notch in the cliff overhang and struck the center of a sun symbol on the left side of the panel. As they watched in awe, the beam pushed the shadow from left to right, slowly bathing the entire message in sunlight like a prehistoric neon sign announcing yet another Christmas, as it has done for centuries. Before their eyes, they had received a message across the ages.

"Subsequent visits showed that the phenomenon only occurred at the winter solstice; and at other times of the year the sun only partially lit the message. In 1985, the distinguished Celtic scholar, Professor Robert T. Meyer visited the site and responded to a question regarding its authenticity in these words: 'Nobody could have faked this sort of thing unless they had a very deep knowledge of Celtic

philosophy, for this is very archaic, and probably from the sixth or seventh centuries. This, for Celtic scholars, is probably at least as important as the discovery of the Dead Sea Scrolls . . . because it shows that Irish Monks, I suppose, came here, I would say, about 1500 years ago.'"

In 1989 lawyers Monroe Oppenheimer and Willard Wirtz wrote an article based on opinions of other archaeologists and linguists experts, disputing the theory that the inscription is written in Ogham script. They further accused Fell of deliberate fraud, a charge Fell denied.

Today, the carvings of the Dingess Petroglyphs remain a controversial mystery.

Are There Still Mountain Lions in Appalachia?

Appalachian Magazine Staff

For countless millennia cougars, also known as mountain lions, pumas, painters and panthers, roamed the Appalachian Mountains of North America. Tales abound of early settlers witnessing panthers drop from virgin forest tree limbs onto unsuspecting individuals below.

Being the fourth-largest cat on the planet, cougars prowled from Alaska to the southern tip of South America, and nearly all places in between, including the entire Appalachian region. Growing to the length of 9 ft. and having the ability t0 leap as far as 15 ft., the intimidating cry of the painter "said to sound like a wailing woman" haunted the dreams of early English inhabitants of the New World.

Indeed, the modern forests of Appalachia are almost unrecognizable compared to the majestic, dense and unimaginably dark woodland that greeted the first white settlers only a handful of centuries ago.

One of the first men to write of the mountain's ancient forests was a young surveyor by the name of George Washington.

Photo: Purportedly taken by a Tennessee Wildlife Resources Trail Cam in Sept. 2015

While plotting the Kanawha River, he wrote in his journal, "Just as we came to the hills, we met with a Sycamore… of a most extraordinary size, it measuring three feet from the ground, forty-five feet round, lacking two inches; and not fifty yards from it was another, thirty-one feet round."

Unfortunately, by 1920, the region, which is now celebrated for its natural beauty, had been reduced to an abhorrent desert, more closely resembling a bombed wasteland than a mountain wonderland described as being "almost heaven."

For the first time in its history, West Virginia was viewed as an eyesore. One visiting writer described the state as "a monotonous panorama of destruction."

A victim of this widespread deforestation, as well as intense hunting, was the region's mountain lion.

Like the Native Americans who were driven westward a century earlier, the panthers of modern-day Virginia, Tennessee, Kentucky and West Virginia, were either pushed west or died at the end of a rifle barrel or due to the scarcity of food.

By the middle of the 1900's, nearly all cougars in the entire state of West Virginia had vanished altogether.

In 2011, the federal Fish and Wildlife Service declared the Eastern Cougar to extinct, recommending that the animal be removed from the nation's endangered species list.

Interestingly, a lingering question still remained: are there really no more wild cougars left in the Appalachian Mountains? The answer to this question was for a while almost as controversial as the Kennedy assassination or the blue and black... I mean white and gold dress that floated around Facebook for months.

Though Eastern Cougars were officially declared extinct, dozens of reported panther sightings throughout the Appalachian Mountains have continued for years.

Just weeks after the Federal government declared Eastern Cougars to be extinct, a cougar was killed by a car in Connecticut. A New York Times article concluded that the cat was not an eastern cougar, but a wild cougar from South Dakota: "Wildlife officials, who at first assumed the cat was a captive animal that had escaped its owners, examined its DNA and concluded that it was a wild cougar from the Black Hills of South Dakota. It had wandered at least 1,500 miles before meeting its end at the front of an S.U.V. in Connecticut. That is one impressive walkabout."

In September 2015, the Tennessee Wildlife Resources Agency reportedly shared a trail camera photo of a passing mountain lion. The confirmation took place in Obion County, which is in western Tennessee, approximately 80 miles west of Nashville and only a few miles east of the Mississippi River on the border of Kentucky.

Regardless of whether the increase in sightings can be attributed to a resurgence of what was believed to be an extinct cat or an invasion of Western Cougars, it is becoming increasingly clear that mountain lions do exist in the wild in the Appalachian Mountains.

Though the odds of you actually coming across a mountain lion while hiking in the Appalachian Mountains are incredibly slim, should you be so unfortunately fortunate, experts give the following advice:

STOP. Do not run, Do not play dead. Do not make any sudden moves. Maintain eye contact and stand tall, looking big and speaking firmly. Throw something NEAR the lion...

Also, you might want to take a picture when safe... because spotting a mountain lion in these parts may be met with the same level of skepticism as making public the UFO you and your buddy spotted that one night!

The Giants of Appalachia
Appalachian Magazine Staff

Ancient writings are filled with references to giants who once lived upon the earth. These references span the globe and encompass nearly all of the world's cultures, ranging from Homer, a Greek poet who lived 400 B.C., to Moses, who wrote of a time before the Great Flood in which "There were giants in the earth in those days..."

Despite the repeated references of a prehistoric time in which the world was inhabited by colossal men, many archeologists and anthropologists have been quick to dismiss these claims, believing instead that the notion of a world once ruled by towering giants was nothing more than an ancient fairytale.

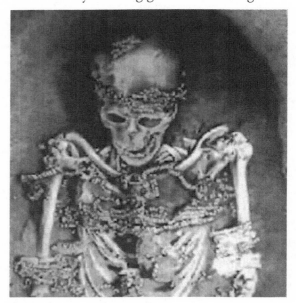

Little publicized discoveries, however, are causing some scientists to take a second look at the idea of a fabled world roamed by giants.

Though knowledge of coal's existence in the Appalachian Mountains had long been held by white settlers, it was not until the late-1800s, during the Industrial Revolution, that the concept of mining and transporting the black ore was deemed feasible.

As the nation entered a new age of manufacturing and growth, the value of coal was quickly realized and the era of widespread Appalachian coal mining commenced.

With armies of men now blasting and digging immeasurably old rock formations, workers began to uncover dozens of strange artifacts – most notably, what appeared to be mega-sized human bones.

On October 13, 1916, The Seattle Star reported that residents in northern Pennsylvania uncovered an Indian burial mound containing the bones of 68 men. According to the article, "The average height of the assembled skeletons was 7 feet, while many were taller. Further evidence of their gigantic size was found in their large stone axes placed in the grave."

The Pennsylvania skeletons are anything but an anomaly. A half-century earlier, workers constructing a bridge in upstate West Virginia were dumbfounded when they dug up three giant skeletons containing strands of reddish hair. A local doctor was called to examine the colossal remains, to which he concluded had to be no shorter than 8' tall and definitely human.

In the fall of 1882, F.M. Fetty and his wife, both amateur archaeologists, were exploring a nearby cliff and found an unusual rock formation along the walls of the shelter. A closer look revealed that a false wall had been erected.

Fetty and his wife remove several of the large stones and made the startling discovery of a giant human mummy a sitting in a chair.

The following summer, James A. Faulkner unearthed an unusually large human skeleton in the same area. A local doctor was called in to measure the skeleton and found it to be at least 7' 4" long.

As similar discoveries were unearthed throughout the Mountain State in the decades to come, public interest picked up, leading the Charleston Daily Mail to publish the following report on October 22, 1922:

"One of the most interesting of the five state parks is Mound Park, at Moundsville from which that city derived its name. Probably no other relic of pre-historic origin has attracted as wide study among archaeologists as the Grave Creeks mound which has given up skeletons of the ancients who constructed it... Archaeologists investigating the mound some years ago dug out a skeleton said to be that of a female because of the formation of the bones. The skeleton was seven feet four inches tall and the jawbone would easily fit over the face of a man weighing 160 pounds."

Tales of colossal giants permeate the American Appalachians and have for centuries haunted the dreams of explorers; however, knowledge of their existence and discoveries has become lost to recent generations — either by design or shear overload of information. Regardless of why, however, scientists are taking a renewed interest in the giants of Appalachia and local residents will probably be hearing a lot more about them in the days to come.

Is There a Lost Silver Mine
Hidden in an Appalachian Cave?
Appalachian Magazine Staff

What if I were to tell you that lost somewhere in the hills of central Appalachia is a forgotten silver mine that is waiting to be discovered?

This may sound like the opening to the latest "National Treasure" movie, but the story actually predates the nation itself by nearly two decades.

As legend tells, a settler named Hans G. Frenchman was captured by Native Americans and taken to a cave somewhere in the mountains of Southwest Virginia where he discovered a rich vein of silver ore.

Frenchman marked the cave's location and later successfully escaped his captors and revealed the location of the mine to Englishman Jonathan Swift.

The two men traveled to the cave and according to legend, took only enough silver to buy two horses, but were unable to locate the mine on a return trip.

In the years ahead, the legend of "Swift's Silver Mine" would take on a life of its own and soon tales of the mine were being recanted in Tennessee, Kentucky and elsewhere in Virginia.

Settlers in Wise County, Virginia, believed that the mine was located on or around Stone Mountain, and that local Indians knew the location of the mine but kept it secret from the white invaders. According to the pioneers, an Indian chief named Benge once said that "if the pale face knew what I knew they could shoe their horses cheaper with silver than with iron."

Two generations later, a famed counterfeiter living in what is now known as Clintwood, Virginia, was rumored to have discovered Swift's mines near Pine Mountain in Southwest Virginia. The counterfeiter was accused of unlawfully striking his own coins (made of pure silver).

According to local legend, the man's "counterfeit" money used more silver, and was worth more, than the official currency at the time. Apparently, the individual mixed the pure silver with other lesser metals to make his money. He never disclosed where he obtained the pure silver, but many people speculated that he found the silver in one of the many caves on Pine Mountain close to his farm.

Other versions of the story place the silver mine farther west than Virginia: Each year in Wolfe County, Kentucky, there is a Swift Silver mine festival in the county seat of Campton, Kentucky where locals believe the mine may be located near Swift Creek.

The Appalachian Mountains have seen more than its fair share of treasure hunters seeking to find Swift's secret stash.

John Filson is the first person known to have referenced the mine following Swift's death. In 1788, Filson claimed a tract of land supposed to have included a silver mine worked by "a certain man named Swift." Filson disappeared, taking with him any knowledge he may have had as to the mine's location.

Kentucky pioneer James Harrod may also have believed in Swift's silver mine. According to Harrod's wife, a man named Bridges claimed to have found the mine, and asked Harrod for his help in developing it. Despite the fact that Harrod and Bridges had a dispute over land some years previous, these two and another man entered the wilderness of Kentucky in 1792, purportedly in search of the mine. Harrod did not return from the trip, and although his body was never found, his wife maintained that Bridges had used the story of the mine to lure him into the woods to murder him.

The Appalachian Mountains of Southwest Virginia and Eastern Kentucky are vast and many areas of the region have not been thoroughly explored in centuries, so who knows, perhaps there is a silver mine hidden in some forgotten and overlooked cave.

Have You Ever Heard of Appalachia's Wampus Cat?

Appalachian Magazine Staff

The dark mountains of Appalachia have lent themselves to mystery and intrigue for centuries — even long before the arrival of European settlers.

Few mountain legends, however, are as riveting and timeless as the story of the "Wampus Cat".

There are two predominate stories surrounding this legend.

The first goes like this: A group of Native American men was set to go out on a long hunting trip. Resentful to the fact that women were not permitted to participate in these expeditions, one of the wives decided to secretly follow the men.

"She cloaked herself in the hide of a cougar and hid near their campfire. Listening to their tales of the hunt, she was soon discovered by the men. Furious that she had violated the secrecy of their hunt, a shaman of the tribe punished the woman by cursing her and making her one with the animal hide she wore. The cursed woman became a half human, half mountain lion beast, forever damned to stalk the woods alone," writes Cryptid Corral.

Another variation of the legend states that an Appalachian village was plagued by stolen livestock.

Believing that a certain woman was a witch, the townspeople followed her to a nearby farm late one night.

"As they watched, the witch transformed into a house cat and snuck into the farmhouse. Inside the house, she spelled the house's sleeping occupants to stay asleep no matter what. Then, she went back out to the barn and began the process of transforming herself back into a woman," writes Catie Rhodes.

As the woman was transforming back into a person, the villagers somehow interrupted the transformation process, leaving the witch half-cat and half-human. "She still wanders the hills, a ghastly half woman-half cat."

"During the 1920s, the men of southwestern Virginia and some parts of northwest Tennessee would use the old tales of the Wampus Cat to their own advantage in a particularly funny way. Whenever an especially good batch of moonshine had been distilled, a shotgun was fired as a signal for the guys to gather up and have a drink of the illegal booze. To avoid suspicion from the womenfolk, the men told their wives that the Wampus Cat had been seen in the area and that they needed to hunt it down and destroy the beast before it could kill or otherwise hurt anything," stated another online article.

The Customer in Dirty Bib Overalls
Appalachian Magazine Staff

In the mountains of Southwest Virginia, there is an old story that has been passed down for generations about a crowded diner in the heart of a small town, a snooty waitress and a customer wearing dirty "bib overalls."

Before we get into the story though, it's probably a good idea to take a moment and explain what a pair of bib overalls actually are, as the working man seems to be an endangered species in modern-day America.

Made of denim, bib overalls are worn over one's clothes and offer an added layer of protection when working outside. They have long been associated with rural men in the Southern United States, especially farmers and railroad workers.

As the story goes, deep in the heart of Carroll County, in Virginia's western panhandle, almost midway between the state lines of West Virginia and North Carolina, an old farmer had been working tirelessly in a hot summer's field.

Hungry, he did something out of character for him — he drove into town and parked his rusted truck alongside the street and proceeded to walk into the most popular dining establishment in town for a quick bite to eat.

As the bell affixed to the door began to clank as it slammed shut behind him, all eyes in the restaurant drew to the old man wearing dirty overalls.

Looking with disgust at the man's grass stains, dirty boots and scraped hands, the folks seated in the booths (wearing their suits and ties) acted as if a hobo had entered the establishment and would attack at any moment.

"I'm sorry sir, but you can't come in here," said the waitress in the most condescending tone she could muster, adding, "You're just too filthy to be seen in a place like this."

A handful of days passed and around lunchtime sometime the following week, the old man climbed back into his puttering old truck and once again drove back into town.

Even dirtier than he was the previous week, the aged farmer once again felt the stares of the entire restaurant as he again heard the door close behind him.

"I've told you sir, you can't eat here. You're just not the type of person we want in this restaurant," said the waitress, this time even more rude than the previous time.

The old man smiled and then said to the woman, "You can't tell me that, because I just fired you."

"What?"

"Last night I closed the deal with the owner of this restaurant and today I am the owner of this establishment, and you're fired."

The entire restaurant looked at the sweaty old farmer wearing a stained up pair of dirty overalls in an entirely new light — he was the richest man in the building.

Indeed, one cannot judge a book by its cover, or a man by his clothes.

Men in denim built this country… men in suits destroyed it.

1874 Report: Stray Bullet Impregnated Virginia Woman During Civil War

Appalachian Magazine Staff

Despite its incalculable tragedy, the American Civil War has provided story-tellers with a lifetime supply of incredible, encouraging and sometimes downright bizarre stories of tragedy and human triumph.

With this being said, it's difficult to imagine any story upping the insanity level of the one published by Dr. Legrand G. Capers in the American Medical Weekly in 1874.

Capers, who served as a field and hospital surgeon during the Civil War for the Confederacy wrote,

"On the 12th day of May, 1863, the battle of R. was fought... Our men were fighting nobly, but pressed by superior numbers, had gradually fallen back to within one hundred and fifty yards of the house. My position being near my regiment, suddenly I beheld a noble, gallant young friend staggering closer, and then fall to the earth. In the same moment a piercing scream from the house reached my ear! I was soon by the side of the young man, and, upon examination, found a compound fracture, with extensive comminution of the left tibia; the ball having ricochetted from these parts, and, in its onward flight, passed through the scrotum, carrying away the left testicle. Scarcely had I finished dressing the wounds of this poor fellow, when the estimable matron came running to me in the greatest

distress, begging me to go to one of her daughters, who, she informed me, had been badly wounded a few minutes before. Hastening to the house, I found that the eldest of the young ladies had indeed received a most serious wound. A minnie ball had penetrated the left abdominal parietes, about midway between the umbilicus and anterior spinal process of the ilium, and was lost in the abdominal cavity, leaving a ragged wound behind. Believing there was little or no hope of her recovery, I had only time to prescribe an anodyne, when our army fell back, leaving both field and village in the hands of the enemy... About six months after her recovery, the movements of our army brought me again to the village of R., and I was again sent for to see the young lady. She appeared in excellent health and spirits, but her abdomen had become enormously enlarged, so much so as to resemble pregnancy at the seventh or eighth month. Indeed, had I not known the family and the facts of the abdominal wound, I should have so pronounced the case. Under the above circumstances, I failed to give a positive diagnosis, determining to keep the case under surveillance... Just two hundred and seventy-eight days from the date of the receipt of the wound by the minnie ball, I delivered this same young lady of a fine boy, weighing eight pounds... About three weeks from the date of this remarkable birth, I was called to see the child, the grandmother insisting there was 'something wrong about the genitals.' Examination revealed an enlarged, swollen, sensitive scrotum, containing on the right side a hard, roughened substance, evidently foreign. I decided upon operating for its removal at once, and in so doing, extracted from the scrotum a minnie ball, mashed and battered as if it had met in its flight some hard, unyielding substance."

There you have it, the world's truly first "son of a gun"!

As you could expect, within a matter of days of this incredible story being published, news of such an exploit had traveled around the globe and Dr. Capers' credibility was lost as medical experts agreed that such a story was simply unbelievable.

Jan Harold Brunvand, author of *Too Good to Be True: The Colossal Book of Urban Legends*, writes that the medical journal was forced to publish a disclaimer to the original article on November 21, 1874: "DR. L.G. CAPERS, of Vicksburg, Miss., disclaims responsibility for the truth of that remarkable case of impregnation by a minnie ball, as reported in No. 19 of this Journal. He tells the story as it was told to him. He does not say it is untrue, but is disposed to appositely remember the truth of the old adage, that 'accidents may happen in the best regulated families.' The joke is, that the Doctor reported the case without any signature, but as the editor is indisposed to be made the victim of canards, and recognized the writing sent, he was unwilling to deprive the author of the contemplated fun, and allowed him to enjoy even more of this than was anticipated. The readers have enjoyed the story much, but not enough 'to cut capers' after reading it."

Due to the fact that the story was first published in a respected medical journal, it was subsequently told and retold for over a century.

To date, this article has been published as fact by Dear Abby, in a 1959 article from the New York State Journal of Medicine, and in the 1981 Farmer's Almanac under the headline, "THE FIRST CASE OF ARTIFICIAL INSEMINATION BY A BULLET".

With so much talk of "Fake News" recently, it may be reassuring to realize that wild Internet rumors have been being believed and circulating around the globe for centuries before the Internet was even invented!

Virginia's Mysterious Devil Monkey Sightings

Appalachian Magazine Staff

The 1990s presented some incredible tales that ranged from the fascinating to downright bizarre throughout many parts of Appalachia. This decade was also known for the introduction of several new mind-altering substances — it remains to be known as to what extent these two facts are related.

At the forefront of the Unsolved Mysteries, made for TV, hair-raising mountain stories was Virginia's Ninth Congressional District — a region known locally as Southwest Virginia.

Though the vast majority of mountain-Virginia's paranormal stories were limited to UFOs, especially silent and stealthy black-triangles that the USAF swore did not exist, the region also showcased a handful of more spine-tingling claims.

At the top of the many twilight tales to spring forth from this decade was one woman's claim to have spotted a mysterious black "devil monkey" in Roanoke, Virginia, in 1994.

According to multiple sources, an Ohio woman was driving through Roanoke around 2:30 a.m. when a construction detour sent her down a dark two-lane country road.

As she drove the wilderness terrain of Southwest Virginia, a creature that looked like a hybrid wolf-monkey leaped in front of her car.

"The creature was all black with very short sleek fur, pointy ears and had a long thin tail. She described it as catlike, and yet not like any cat she had ever seen... The creature was very tall, because she saw it when it was standing on its hind legs and was easily 6 feet tall. She indicated its torso looked very much like that of a very thin man and its head resembled a man almost with a pointy beard. However, the creature's hind legs were like a wild cat or dog. It was very muscular and thin," writes one source.

The woman later shared her story with US Game & Wildlife officials who insisted it must have been a feral dog or wolf, but the woman was emphatic that the creature she saw was neither of the two.

A few weeks following the woman's ordeal, livestock in the area around the location where the alleged incident took place began disappearing.

Granted, this seems like a bizarre story that could easily be attributed to midnight AM talk radio and a case of some bad gas station coffee; however, it is interesting to note that only two decades earlier, just down I-81 in Smyth County's Saltville, Virginia, various individuals claimed to have spotted nearly the exact same creature.

In 1959, a couple driving down a back road in Saltville, Virginia, reportedly had their car attacked by a large, powerful creature they claimed chased their vehicle and left deep scratches along the door.

"According to their account, an ape-like beast attacked their car, leaving three scratch marks on the vehicle... [the couple's daughter] described the terrifying attacker: 'It had light, taffy colored hair, with a white blaze down its neck and underbelly... it stood on two, large well-muscled back legs and had shorter front legs or arms.'"

A handful of years later, an almost exact same claim was made in the Smyth County, Virginia, community when two nurses from the Saltville area were driving home from work one morning and were attacked by an unknown creature who reportedly ripped the convertible top from their car. Luckily the nurses — though surely frightened out of their wits — were unharmed.

The mysterious monkey-wolf hybrid beast would come to be known as "the devil monkey" and in the decades that followed, numerous alleged sightings of these animals were reported.

In recent years, devil monkey sightings have waned, but from time to time, an occasional sighting of these mysterious creatures is quietly whispered about in corner barbershops or over an Appalachian campfire.

Mountain Voices:
Reader & Staff Opinions

Finding my Religion in Rural Appalachia

Written by Jordan Ball

My grandfather, "Poppy" Gene Jackson, found Jesus Christ when he was a couple years younger than I am now and earned a reputation as a straight shooter who preached up and down every holler in the coalfields of Mingo County, West Virginia. As he tells it, the reputation earned him praise from some, and disdain from others. Some folks couldn't handle his sermons, and he was sometimes not invited back to the pulpit. That's the cost of telling the truth, he says. The truth sometimes isn't popular. I recently learned this when I started to preach the gospel – not of Jesus Christ – but of the beauties and complexities of rural Appalachians.

Rural Appalachia, seemingly a land of forgotten men and women, was re-discovered by authors, journalists, and pundits after last year's stunning political upset. After decades of being largely ignored, residents have suddenly been confronted by opinions of scorn, antipathy, and occasional empathy from the average outsider. This has led many rural Appalachians to wonder: why did they forget about us?

If you take a trip from Pittsburgh, Pennsylvania, to Williamson, West Virginia, you'll venture through resilient, diverse communities that have long confronted condescension from outsiders. I embark on the 309-mile trip twice a month, racing coal trains through the mountainous terrain, into the heart of the Billion-Dollar Coal Field, where I am an adopted son. When I arrive, I am immediately met with a sense of community and family, and I ponder to myself: why did they forget my people?

Butcher Holler gave us Loretta Lynn, who empowered women with songs like "The Pill". The West Virginia-Kentucky border was a battleground for the infamous Hatfield and McCoy feud, and the region cultivated pioneers like Mother Jones, a dressmaker turned organizer, who mobilized working men and women around worker's rights. The United Mine Workers stared down militarized resistance in Morewood, Pennsylvania, and miners from Southeast Ohio to Northern Alabama dug the coal that created the steel that built great American cities. During the 20th Century, tours of economically distressed communities like Inez, Kentucky by LBJ gave a face to federal anti-poverty programs also spearheaded by FDR and JFK, and the region has since become home to some of the world's most consequential poets, artists, scientists, engineers, doctors, educators, and entrepreneurs.

Although my parents left Mingo County and moved me around big cities, I haven't been able to stay away from my rural roots. It was in the coalfields where I learned how to drive and how to shoot a gun. It's where I learned how to climb a mountain by foot and four-wheeler, and had my first real heartbreak. It's where Aunt Darlene let me shadow her in the ER for a day, so I could witness a doctor re-attach a severed limb. It's where I learned that wealth doesn't have to be material, because those with little means can have an abundance of happiness. It's where I developed a sincere appreciation for hard work, rugged individualism, biscuits and gravy, coal, and banjo pickin'. Most of all, it's where I learned and earned my independence.

So after deep reflection and countless conversations with people of many political persuasions, I am convinced that many outsiders didn't just forget about the good people of rural Appalachia; many abandoned them as well.

It's disheartening to see that renewed interest in Appalachia is sometimes accompanied by both blatant and inferred disrespect for coal miners and their profession. Whether it's the activists who insist that recognizing the dignity of mining is "romanticizing nostalgia", or the politician who refuses to pass legislation that funds a miner's health care or pension, our miners deserve better. Just as harmful is the uninspired comedian who stereotypes a diverse region as filled with homogenous, toothless, and racist people, or a journalist who defines rural communities only as opioid-riddled and economically distressed, without giving consideration to the vibrancy, entrepreneurship, and development that continues to transform the region. It's the continual broad brushing, vilification, and defamation by those that are convinced that hard working men and women in rural America are motivated by malice that first offends Appalachians, and then leads to anger. So, is it any wonder that they reached their limits and flipped over the table?

But for every naysayer and critic, there are many well-meaning people whose empathy and intellectual curiosity reaffirm my faith in humanity. Many friends, peers, and colleagues are eager to challenge themselves to engage with folks they previously felt they couldn't understand. And, of course there are some politicians, journalists, and ordinary Americans who have "gotten it" all along.

Rural Appalachians are responding with a clear message: Come visit our communities. Listen. Learn. We're strong, diverse, and resilient people. We aren't waiting for Superman, for our communities are already comprised of fighters – young and old, progressive and conservative, wealthy and poor, and people of all stripes, creeds, ethnicities, and religions – who work tirelessly to raise healthy families, develop strong communities, and yes – build the nation.

So like my grandfather, a fearless truth-teller and the greatest preacher I've ever known, I will continue to preach the gospel of Appalachia as I know it, and fight for my people, despite potential criticism. In the process of falling in love with my roots, I found my religion and purpose. This summer, the fiery preacher from Williamson, West Virginia who was saved in 1959, will baptize his grandson – me – in 2017, in the hollers that cultivated generations upon generations of our family. And as an adopted son of the coalfields, this is something I will never forget.

Jordan Ball, 26 years old, is a United States Senate regional representative, Co-Director of New Leaders Council Pittsburgh, and an advocate for Appalachia. He has been featured in local and national publications, including "100 Days in Appalachia", and was recognized in 2017 as a leading regional influencer by Pittsburgh's "The Incline".

Create a National Park in McDowell County, W.Va.

Written by Garret Mathews

When I left the region 30 years ago, McDowell County was in critical condition. In some areas, the unemployment rate was more than 80 percent. Indeed, it was easier to count the number of men and women who had jobs. People were moving out in droves, leaving behind scores of abandoned houses and boarded-up storefronts.

Today, the place is on life support with little hope that coal can make a comeback, and almost no chance that any other industry will sprout roots and pick up the slack. There is no four-lane highway in McDowell County. No chain restaurants. No chain motels.

In the early 1950s – before mine mechanization – around 100,000 folks lived in these mountains. Now, it's closer to 22,000. More than 50 percent of McDowell County residents have annual incomes below $25,000. One in three lives in poverty. Internet service is limited. Telephone service is spotty.

It's almost impossible to attract professional people because of the lack of decent housing. The overwhelming majority of school children qualify for free lunch.

I have a deep affection for McDowell County and return occasionally to drive the twisty backroads. This helps me remember the plucky folks who, decades ago, told a green writer their stories of hand-loading coal onto wagons pulled by mules, and how they survived mine explosions that killed dozens of their comrades.

If this part of the country hasn't been beaten down enough by a battered economy, a new scourge has popped up since my last byline appeared in the Daily Telegraph.

Drugs, mostly methamphetamine and OxyContin. McDowell County leads the state in the number of overdose deaths. A good chunk of residents don't bother looking for work because they know they can't pass the employer's drug test.

Many who remain in the Free State, as it's known, are dependent on federal aid. Infrastructure is aging. Raw sewage gurgles next to decrepit mobile homes. Clean water is at a premium.

The cost to maintain McDowell County as it is – never mind making improvements – is staggering and will only get worse.

Why not consider something new?

Why not consider turning part of McDowell County into a national park that would celebrate the area's rich mining history?

Many buildings from coal's glory days are still in place. Refurbish them. Add signage and costumed interpreters to tell visitors about the shaft elevators, the preparation plants and the maze of underground pathways.

Recreate a bathhouse. Explain how each coal digger had his own tag so the checkweighman would know how much product the guy shoveled during the shift.

The remnants of several coal camps are still in place, and some come complete with tipples. In most cases, the company stores are long gone. No worries. Build replicas. Explain how mine owners controlled every aspect of their employees' lives from the houses they lived in to where they got groceries. Invest in piles of faux scrip to pass out to the kids.

Back in the day, national attention turned to McDowell County when the contract between the coal operators and the United Mine Workers expired. Some strikes lasted months and there was picket-line violence between the opposing sides. Construct informational kiosks at some of the hotspots.

Visitors will need lodges and restaurants. Build on site. Hire locals to run them.

Yes, many families will be forced to relocate, but there is precedent for such action.

In 1926, a bill was signed by President Calvin Coolidge that provided for the establishment of the Great Smoky Mountains National Park in East Tennessee. The legislature appropriated funds for land acquisition. Additional money was raised by wealthy individuals and private groups. School children famously pledged their pennies.

The park was dedicated in 1940. Millions of people visit every year. A once-downtrodden region is now on solid footing.

McDowell County was once the largest coal producer in West Virginia. Those days are gone. What's needed is a Plan B. A nice, green one.

The words "tourism" and "Free State" have rarely been used in the same sentence.

Maybe that time has come..

Garret Mathews wrote feature stories and, later, columns for the Bluefield, W. Va., Daily Telegraph from 1972 until 1987 when he was hired to write the metro column for the Evansville, Ind., Courier & Press. His legacy website – www.pluggerpublishing.com — (Folks Are Talking) features dozens of pieces he wrote for the Bluefield newspaper. The Telegraph's circulation area takes in McDowell County, one of the poorest counties in the United States.

America's Greatest Problem:
We've Been Off the Farm Too Long
Appalachian Magazine Staff

This year, our nation will celebrate its 241st birthday and though my heart fills with patriotic fervor each time I catch a glimpse of those red stripes flapping in the wind, I can't help but have those feelings checked by the harsh understanding that America 2016 is a nation in dire trouble.

Far from being the land of the free and the home of the brave, we are now a nation of spineless weaklings ready to be offended at the drop of a hat and often it is the very ones who dropped the hat who are the most offended.

I do not pretend to be an expert on sociology or American history – everything I know I had to learn from my life's experiences, mostly as a child on a +200-acre beef farm in nowhere Virginia. The older I get, the more I have come to realize, however, that it was here that I received the type of education no Ivy League institution can come close to offering. My only regret is that 200 million other American children never had the same opportunities I enjoyed – opportunities to bottle feed a baby calf, drive a truck through an empty field at the age of 5 (alone), spend summers sitting alongside my father inside the cab of a John Deere tractor, begin Christmas morning the same way I began every other cold and windy winter morning – opening the gates for dad as he unrolled hay for hundreds of hungry animals.

In the year 1790, 90% of the American population were farmers. By 1850, this percentage had dropped to 64%, and then down to only 21% by the year 1930. Today, only 2% of the American population serve as farmers.

And though American agriculture is more productive than ever, I'm afraid that as a nation we are beginning to witness the consequences of having raised multiple generations who have never looped a metal chain through a gate or chased lightning bugs through a field of freshly mowed hay.

As a nation, we have allowed Disney to convince our children that all animals are cute and cuddly, then wonder why dozens of people get killed each year attempting to take selfies with grizzly bears, cougars and copperheads.

As a nation, we have replaced the garden hoe and watering bucket with an Xbox and cell phone, then wonder why our "children" refuse to move out at the age of 30.

As a nation, the vast majority of our families have never even came across an injured bird, let alone taken the time to nurse one back to health, then we wonder why a generation has been brought up to have no respect for nature or its Creator.

While our forebears were busy praying for rain, we have come to regard the water that falls from the sky as being a cursed object — unaware that it is the rain that keeps us fed each day... All sunshine and no rain makes a barren desert, but hardly anyone realizes this in 2016 America; which is why so many never find peace during their darkest days.

There was a time when Americans consumed bacon, sausage, biscuits, gravy, fried eggs and a big glass of milk each morning — and yet they rarely got fat. Why? Because after eating such a hardy breakfast, they went out in the fields and spent the next thirteen hours fixing fences, hanging gates, delivering calves, killing, yes, killing predators, and harvesting food.

Farm work is dirty, tiring, sometimes cruel and always difficult; which is exactly why the percentage of Americans who engage in this work has declined with every generation.

Yet, it was this type of upbringing that allowed a nation to produce men and women who pulled together to fend off the forces of Hell in the Second World War, explore the heavens, eradicate disease and tap the ocean depths.

Sadly, those farm children are dying off the scene each day. They have been replaced by "men" who have never gotten dirt under their fingernails and purchase overpriced coffee as a status symbol.

I'm not so foolish to believe that all of our ills could be solved by a trip back to the farm, but I am confident that if a few more people had the type of upbringing I enjoyed, the world would have a lot more common sense!

"Men In Denim Built Our Country...Men In Suits Destroyed It."

Appalachian Values
Learned from my People on the Tug
Written by Dr. Donna L. Burgraff, Ohio University

Photo: Garland Harper, the station agent at Williamson, West Virginia, points out the high water mark of floods in April 1977. Muddy water covered the station up to eight feet high, but Harper had the station running again within a few days of the flood receding. Harper was a native of Lynchburg, Virginia; he lived at the station during his 5-day shifts.

Dr. Burgraff is an Associate Professor at Ohio University. She currently resides in Chillicothe, Ohio. Dr. Burgraff has shared her proud Appalachian Heritage around world during her leadership fellowship through the W. K. Kellogg Foundation.

It was still dark outside and I was sound asleep when my bedroom light flipped on. It has been over 40 years now, so I cannot remember exactly what my mom said but her intentions were clear. I was still groggy, for we had been out until after midnight the night before helping our friends and neighbors. I can remember thinking as I got dressed, "What did she say was happening? Where did she go?" It was the morning of April 4, 1977.

I walked out on our front porch where my dad was sitting. He was clearly in a state of shock. As I looked down the street the sun was just rising and I could see it. A wall of water about six feet high was steadily moving down our street. I knew two things. The Tug Fork River was going to invade our home, and at the rate it was moving we had about an hour before it did.

Appalachian Value # 1: Help others whenever you can.

It had rained like "cats and dogs" the day before. So, the entire Tug Valley Area knew that flooding in the low lying areas was going to happen. That is why we had been out past midnight. Two relatively young parents with two teenagers and their friends could definitely help, especially a single mother with young children or an elderly widow. It is just what you do for, as the Good Book says, to whom much is given much is required. After all, we lived well above the flood plain, at least until then.

What we did not know was that 15 ½ inches of rain had fallen in 30 hours in a place we had never heard of—Jolo, West Virginia. This little town sits at the headwaters of the Tug River. The Tug would end up, when it was all over, putting over 20 feet of water into the towns in Mingo County, West Virginia and Pike County, Kentucky. We were, in effect, doomed even as we helped others. We just did not know it.

Appalachian Value # 2: When life gets tough, so do you.

I left the front porch and went back into the house. Mom was coming in the back door. She had taken our car "up on the hill" as we called it. We lived at the foot of Slater Street in Williamson, WV. Slater Street climbs directly up the side of an Appalachian mountain. About ¾ of the way up the mountain sits the city's cemetery. As the water moved in, the entire neighborhood had taken their cars and parked them one behind the other in the road that ran through the cemetery. Mom's quick action had saved our car just in time.

I met her in the kitchen and tears welled up in my eyes. I still remember her exact words, "No time for crying now. We'll cry later." That was enough to stop the tears and get to work. Mom got out the garbage bags, and she handed me one and said to fill it full of clothes. Someone also went out back and got our metal garbage cans and dumped the garbage out.

My Mem-maw lived in a house just as you entered the cemetery. Mom's intent was clear.

We were going to save what we could.

Appalachian Value # 3: Do not let others stop you (even those you love) from doing what needs to be done.

We got right to work. As we did, Dad kept walking around like what is probably best described as a zombie. He kept saying that there was no need to pack things up. The water was not going to get into the house.

I remember thinking that I did not know what he was looking at because it was clear the water was going to flood the house. He would say, "If it gets up one more step." Well, it more than did.

Mom did not let Dad's state of shock stop her. She told him to just go sit down that "me and the girls got this." So back out on the porch he went while we continued throwing things into garbage bags and cans.

Appalachian Value # 4: Things that mean the most really are those that money cannot buy.

Once we got a load ready, Mom said "Take this to Mem-maw's". So, there we went my sister and me on each side of that metal garbage can. We had the handle in one hand and a garbage bag in the other carrying our family's belongings up on the hill. We were 14 and 16 at the time.

As soon as we got there, we dropped the load on Mem-maw's porch and headed back down the hill to get another. We carried as many loads as we could before the water overtook the house. Through Mom's efforts that day we saved most of our clothes, what food we had in the cabinets and refrigerator, and our most precious belongs. In those garbage cans were yearbooks, baby photos, family albums. When you only have an hour, those are the things you save.

The water eventually stopped rising later that day but not before 33 inches were in the house destroying pretty much everything. Very little was spared that day in our neighborhood: one church; the homes on Slater Street hill, luckily my Mem-maw's being one of them; and the grade school.

Appalachian Value # 5: No matter how bad it is, someone is always worse off.

We were cut off from the rest of the world. The entire valley was flooded. We had no electricity, no water, no heat and the temperature had dropped and it started to snow. Someone had opened the grade school for shelter and offered up its kitchen contents for the neighborhood. My family members went down and came back with lots of those little milk cartons. There were over 25 people seeking refuge at Mem-Maw's. We needed a lot of that milk, but we did not need it all. Dad and Mom took a blanket put those milks in the center and sent my sister and me around the cemetery.

We may not have had a bed at Mem-maw's, but at least we had a roof over our heads. Many of our neighbors were taking refuge in their cars. There we went, each holding two corners of that blanket with little grade school milks in the center. We went car to car through the cemetery knocking on car windows offering milk to those less fortunate on what was, for us, the worst day of our lives.

Appalachian Value #6: There comes a time to sit down and cry; then you get back up.

Once the water went down, the clean-up began. Flood mud was a new term I learned. And, oh the smell! Words cannot describe the smell.

Dad eventually got back to his usual self almost as soon as the house was flooded. He led our family's clean-up effort

One day, a couple of weeks after the water went down, I was in the house alone working on cleaning up our living room paneling—a chore my mom and dad left me with. We had a good sized living room with dark brown paneling. I was on my hands and knees cleaning from the waterline down. I scrubbed and scrubbed until all of that flood mud was gone.

When I finished the entire room, I stood up and admired my work. Then I saw it. Slowly at first and then it worked its way around the room like dominos falling. The flood mud was seeping back onto the paneling. Pretty soon it looked like I had not even done a thing.

It was at that moment I just sat down on the plywood that was now our living room floor and just cried my eyes out. I felt if anyone had a right to feel sorry for herself it was my sixteen-year-old self who had just worked so hard and had nothing to show for it. After a few minutes passed, I picked myself up off the floor, took the bucket outside and got some fresh water and started again.

That paneling had to be cleaned four times before the mud stopped seeping out. Even though I have not lived in that house for over twenty-five years now, I could walk up to the wall in that living room and put my hand on it exactly where the flood line started.

Appalachian Value # 7: Find humor in all things

Five days after the flood was Easter Sunday. The only church that had not been flooded in the neighborhood invited everyone to services, come as you are. Mom decreed we were going to church. "Church!?" I thought. What in the world was she thinking? We had been cleaning up flood mud for three days with no water to clean ourselves up. Mom insisted. She said that Calvary Baptist was going to allow women into the sanctuary in pants and that was something we were not going to miss. (In 1977 this was earthshattering for sure). I guess we would take a stand for women's equality!

As we were getting ready, Mom came out of the bedroom flipping a yellow bandanna singing at the top of her lungs, "Put on Your Easter Bonnet. With All the Frills Upon It. You'll Be the Grandest Lady in the Easter Parade."

Appalachian Value # 8: Always take time to Praise the Lord!

Down the hill we went. Each of us in a different colored bandanna over hair that had not been washed in almost a week, in clothes we had dug out of garbage bags. Dare I say we had an Easter parade like no other. We worshiped together with our neighbors, even in our pants. Somehow I know the Lord did not mind. We celebrated Easter, mourned all we had lost, and praised God who had spared our lives but not our homes.

Appalachian Value # 9: Love will see you through

I left my Appalachian home two years after the "Great Flood of '77" to go to college. I went out into a world that made fun of the way I talked and let me know that where I was from was a place that people in the world found no value in. "Poor, Dumb Hillbilly" is the stereotype. I have often had the opportunity to speak to groups all across the country and I tell them, "Yep, that's me."

Every stereotype that you can think of, I am it. My bloodline traces back to one of the defendants of the Matewan Massacre and to the McCoys, yes the ones of Hatfields and McCoys fame. While others not from these mountains cannot understand it, I know that the values I learned, quite literally on the Tug River, are good values, solid values.

During the flood's aftermath, I saw a few examples of the worst of humankind, but they really were very few. Mostly, I saw neighbors helping neighbors. I saw strangers become instant friends. I saw families, like mine, that stuck together and got through an awful time. Mostly, I saw the love of a people for each other and the good Lord above. This love was certainly put to a test when that river left its banks, but it never faltered.

I do not talk about the spring/summer of 1977 much. I do not really like to think about it. When I do, I think about all the things my mother taught me during those dark days. These were values Mem-maw had taught her and Mommy before her. Values borne out of hardship in a region often maligned in this country, these are Appalachian values, and I do thank God every day that I have them and do my best to personify them.

Dr. Burgraff is an Associate Professor at Ohio University. She currently resides in Chillicothe, Ohio. Dr. Burgraff has shared her proud Appalachian Heritage around world during her leadership fellowship through the W. K. Kellogg Foundation.

Before You Make that Next West Virginia Joke, Consider These Facts

Appalachian Magazine Staff

In modern-day America, there are few things that are as socially unacceptable and career-ending as making fun of someone based on their race or place of origin... that is unless of course your target happens to be from West Virginia, in which case, the very ones who seem most offended by similar jokes directed at other peoples are often the ringleaders in asking if someone has all their teeth or has sexual relations with their sister. Funny thing, that hypocrisy stuff.

I know this to be a fact because I am from West Virginia and I experience this reality on a near-daily basis.

"Okay, I just need you to write your place of birth right here," said the woman hiring me for a job. Five seconds later: "Ha, you're from West Virginia... you got all your teeth?"

Stopping for gas in a destitute southern city: Guy climbs out of a car that is literally bungee corded together and says to me, "I'm surprised they let you backwards hicks out..." as he points to the West Virginia license plate on my vehicle worth ten-times the amount of his (I say this not being prideful, but simply to point out the absurdity of the situation).

Or my personal favorite: a Georgia shopkeeper asked to see my driver's license and then proceeded to rehearse the same old worn out West

Virginia jokes I've heard my entire life — and so has every other West Virginian — "What do you call a full set of teeth... why are one of your legs longer than the other... why do birds fly upside down over West Virginia..." and of course a few cousin comments. After his limited intellect finally reached the point where he was able to realize I was growing irritated, he attempted to rebound by saying something to the effect of, "Oh buddy, I'm just kidding with you. I've got family who live in Richmond, so I love West Virginia."

Now don't get me wrong, I'm one of the most fun-loving individuals you will ever meet and I'm always up for a good laugh; however, I just don't think that making jokes about someone raping their sister is all that funny, or for that matter reflects well upon the intelligence level of the individual making said "joke."

With all of this said, the next time you may be inclined to tell a West Virginia joke to some new fella you just met, here are a few questions you may want to ask yourself first:

Is there a chance they've already heard this worn out joke a thousand times already?

Keep in mind that though this may be the first West Virginian you've seen in a while (since you probably don't get out much) the West Virginian you have encountered obviously does get out, seeing that they've traveled to wherever you are, and whatever joke it is that you are about to tell, chances are they've heard it a dozen times before you and you're probably not nearly as talented at telling it as the last person!

With this said, never forget, first impressions last a lifetime and you're about to absolutely ruin your first impression.

Am I being a hypocrite?

If you'd never in a million years be willing to crack a Mexican joke or a Chinese joke or an African joke to someone you just met from one of those places, mocking their accent or how poor their homeplace is, why in the world is it suddenly okay for you to do so to someone who happens to hail from West Virginia?

Am I even familiar with West Virginia?

Born in the midst of the American Civil War, partly out of a desire to oppose the commonly accepted notion that it was perfectly alright for one human to own another, the State of West Virginia boasts a proud history that embodies so much of what is great about America.

Is it your policy to make fun of people who happen to be from the state that had more deaths per capita than any other state in the Union during the Vietnam War?

Is it your policy to make fun of people who happen to be from the same place as legendary folks such as Don Knotts, Homer Hickam, Chuck Yeager, Brad Paisley, Jessica Lynch, Jerry West, T.D. Jakes, John F. Nash, and John Henry?

Is it your policy to make fun of people who happen to be from the state that literally offered up the timber and energy that built much of the nation during the late 1800s and early 1900s?

Each time our nation's citizens have been summoned to give testimony of their national loyalty, West Virginia parents have offered their children as a sacrifice upon the altar of freedom for a country of which half the population seems to have trouble even remembering the state exists and the other half begins a litany of worn out jokes at the very mention of this place.

The people of West Virginia have watched as Washington politicians destroyed everything they had worked to create for over a century and a half, yet still have the decency and love for country to line their bumpy streets with coal dust saturated American flags and teach their children to sing 'God Bless America.'

I hope, for your sake, you heed my unsolicited advice the next time you meet someone from West Virginia and rather than telling some offensive joke about a full set of teeth, instead compliment them for being from such a wild and wonderful place. If you do this, you will leave them stunned (because they're already bracing themselves for the typical blah blah blah).

After they get over being stunned that you actually had something nice to say about their home state, you will have found a loyal friend for life – and that my friend, is priceless.

West Virginia: The State That Got Bought

Appalachian Magazine Staff

The existence of coal in West Virginia had been known by European colonists since the mid-1700s. Early settlers to the region were even said to have extracted ground layers of the soft rock for use in heating their homes.

Still, the first large scale mining of coal in West Virginia did not begin until the early-1830s and existed merely as a support to the region's booming salt industry.

West Virginia's first true coal miners were slaves who extracted the mineral for use as a fuel to fire nearby salt furnaces. These furnaces were mostly located along the Kanawha River.

According to Ronald L. Lewis, professor of history emeritus at West Virginia University, "The erection of salt furnaces in Kanawha County beginning in 1797 provided the initial stimulus to coal mining. By 1840, 90 furnaces produced a million bushels of salt annually and consumed 200,000 tons of coal."

Prior to the American Civil War, the demand for salt began to decline; however, bituminous coal (soft coal) had proven itself as being an economic alternative to burning wood.

In the days leading up to the Lincoln Presidency, western Virginia coal was being used to power steamboats floating along the Ohio River, in coal oil lamps and in factories scattered across the northeast.

The outbreak of the Civil War severely crippled the region's coal industry, as western Virginia soon found itself at the epicenter of a tug-of-war game being played between the ruling elite in Richmond and Wheeling. In the end, the State of West Virginia was formed in June 1863.

As the nation entered into the industrial revolution, the limitless resources of West Virginia's coal and timber seemed irresistible to many of the nation's wealthiest companies.

The late Matewan resident, Joseph P. Garland, stated that his grandfather, who was illiterate, was tricked into giving up 1,666 acres of the family's land for a single shotgun.

"They've [southern West Virginians] been robbed, raped and cheated out of their land," stated Garland.

Despite the state's incredible wealth, few natives were ever able to enjoy much gain from the rich resources abounding in the area, as outside corporations quickly gobbled up much of the territory of southern West Virginia.

Aided by the natural transportation route provided by the Tug River, outside loggers moved into the area and cleared many of the county's most valuable woodland.

The arrival of the N&W Railroad allowed for the timber to be shipped east, further accelerating the rate of the state's deforestation.

At the turn of the century, non-residents owned over half the land in Mingo County, West Virginia; as was the case in several other coalfield counties.

Observing this problem, William MacCorkle, West Virginia Governor, warned the state legislature in his inaugural address on March 4, 1893, that "the state is rapidly passing under the control of large foreign and non-resident landowners." He cautioned that "the men who are today purchasing the immense acres of the most valuable lands in the state are not citizens and have only purchased in order that they may carry to their distant homes in the North the usufruct of the lands of West Virginia."

MacCorkle, the son of a Confederate Major and sixth consecutive Democratic governor of West Virginia witnessed his dire warning prove true.

Within seven years, destructive logging techniques had removed half of the state's forests. Nearly all of the state's timber resources had been exhausted within two decades.

For the first time in history, West Virginia was viewed as an eyesore. One visiting writer described the state as, "a monotonous panorama of destruction."

Ronald Eller, a professor of history at the University of Kentucky describes the effects of 'absentee landownership' in the following way:
"Because of absentee ownership of the state's resources, the dollars that could have built better schools and better roads and better health services in the early part of the century flowed out of the region and we got what we call 'growth without development.' We got a short period of immense growth and expansion and boom period and jobs, but we didn't get the development of those aspects that will sustain a community over time and provide a quality of life."

Submit Your Articles

We're always eager to share the opinions and views of our readers, unfortunately, *Appalachian Magazine* is unable to pay writers at this time... Hopefully this will change soon!

Writers who wish for *Appalachian Magazine* to publish their work are encouraged to submit their manuscripts to:
publisher@appalachianmagazine.com,
with "ARTICLE SUBMISSION" written in the subject line.

The ideal article length is between 750 to 2,000 words; however, other works will be considered. Also, include your name and a brief author bio (2-3 sentences).

Appalachian Magazine reserves the right to refuse to publish any submission and by submitting a work, you are authorizing *Appalachian Magazine* to republish the manuscript on any and all platforms the company desires.

Please allow up to one week for a response from the time your article was submitted.

We look forward to hearing from you!

Appalachia's Plight, Blight & Shining Light

Life Expectancy in Appalachia is Actually Dropping
Appalachian Magazine Staff

In May 2017, the National Institutes of Health (NIH) published research stating that as a whole, Americans are living longer than ever before; sadly, this fountain of youth is not available to everyone, in fact, it has bypassed the millions of Americans who call the mountains of Appalachia home.

We knew things were getting bad for the residents of abandoned ghost towns in forgotten coalfield counties, but today's data paints a picture of just how bad: Life expectancies in many parts is actually dropping.

"Depending on where you live in this great country, life expectancy can vary more than 20 years—a surprisingly wide gap that has widened significantly in recent decades," stated Dr. Francis Collins of the NIH.

According to Collins, researchers attribute this disturbing gap to a variety of social and economic influences, as well as differences in modifiable behavioral and lifestyle factors, such as obesity, inactivity, and tobacco use.

A study published in JAMA Internal Medicine found that the average American baby born in 2014 can expect to live to about age 79. That's up from a national average of about 73 in 1980 and around 68 in 1950. However, babies born in many parts of Eastern Kentucky can expect to live only about 70 years. That's in stark contrast to a child born about 300 miles away in Fairfax County, Virginia, where life expectancy at birth now exceeds age 83.

Dozens of Appalachian counties saw their life expectancies remain unchanged or even drop between 1987 and 2007 and thirteen counties across the United States actually have lower life expectancies today than they did in 1980. Life expectancy in Owsley County, Kentucky, for example, dropped from age 72 to age 70.

A lot of these troubling statistics can be attributed to what seems to be a rise in deaths among adults aged 25 to 45 — more than 1 in 10 U.S. counties saw an increased risk of death for adults in this age group.

The differences in life span across the country can be explained in part by socioeconomic factors, including race, education, and income, and access to health care. But nearly three-fourths of the variation in longevity is accountable to behavioral and metabolic risk factors, including obesity, exercise, smoking, alcohol and drug addiction, blood pressure, and diabetes.

To put it simply, residents of Appalachia are dying off and we're doing it quicker than ever before. And if we're going to be honest, a lot of the blame is our own fault.

Sure, not everyone has the money to purchase organic greens from their local farmers market (and yes, this capability certainly helps a lot in living long and healthy lives), but in the same token, no one is forcing the people of our communities to dump energy drinks into alcohol or mix bath chemicals together. This may not be popular preaching, but it's the truth and with statistics like these, this isn't the time to mince words.

A lot of talk has been placed on what we need to do in order to turn the communities of Appalachia around, but the reality is we may need to back up from this approach and begin working on ourselves first. Before we can begin making major changes to entire towns, we may need to begin making even more major changes in our personal lives. Failure for us to begin doing so may end in us simply not being around much longer.

I love the people of my home and pray for the situations of so many to improve on a daily basis, but if lasting changes are to be made, it's going to begin with each person deciding they're tired of business as usual and being willing to begin major changes in their own personal lives.

Interstate 73:
The Best Hope for Southern West Virginia
Appalachian Magazine Staff

Photo: I-73 End in North Carolina, courtesy: Washuotaku

In 2014, the West Virginia legislature voted to name Take Me Home Country Roads an official state song.

Though the folks in the Mountain State love singing this John Denver classic at Mountaineer Field in Morgantown, 170 miles to the south, the residents of what was formerly known as "coal country" have had just about as much as they can handle of their country roads.

Long before the time when Jay Rockefeller lived in the Governor's Mansion and yard signs could be spotted throughout Mingo County declaring, "these roads could 'rock-a-feller'", residents of Southern West Virginia have been fighting and scraping for basic infrastructure — especially when it comes to their country roads.

In the 1970s, things became so dire, that residents in the tiny community of Vulcan even went so far as to petition the Soviet Union for foreign aid during the height of the Cold War in order to get a broken down bridge replaced. The bridge served as the only entrance and exit to their tiny village, yet state leaders seemed disinterested in fixing the structure until the nation's sworn enemy used the event to internationally shame America and the Mountain State.

The latter half of the 20th century was difficult for this region, as dozens of counties were forced to harvest the fruits of more than a century's worth of absentee landownership and a universal mindset that seemed to view the state's southern counties with little more regard than how a 19th century empire saw distant mineral colonies; colonies and peoples created for the sole purpose of making fat cats in far away cities even wealthier.

A testament to this failed system can be spotted along the pathway of US Route 52: Once a busy thoroughfare that linked the Upper Midwest to the Southland, the winding dusty road is now a panorama of destruction for countless miles. Until one has witnessed this "American carnage" firsthand, views that more closely resemble scenes from the latest apocalyptic Hollywood thriller than an American community, it is impossible for he or she to understand just how catastrophic things in this forgotten region of the nation have become.

To put the carnage into perspective, McDowell County had 98,887 residents in 1950. In 2015, that number had withered to 25,292.

In 2015, McDowell County had the highest rate of drug-induced deaths of any county in the entire nation, with 141 deaths per 100,000 people — ten times the national average. Neighboring Wyoming County, West Virginia, had the second highest rate in the country.

Sadly, these problems aren't unique to one or two localities. The level of misery in many places of the Mountain State has reached a whole new level. According to the U.S. Department of Commerce, the entire state is estimated to have lost a net total of 9,951 residents between 2015 and 2016. This equates to a net loss of 27 individuals each day.

Why? Why are drugs running rampant and the general populace so miserable in many places of a state that is so beautiful? Perhaps this is oversimplifying the solution just a little, but not by much, but the simple answer is that there truly aren't any jobs for people to work in this region and as a result, the average person has one of three options: 1.) settle for a terrible job that doesn't pay well, generally great distances away; 2.) drown their sorrows and misery in any substance available; or 3.) get out of dodge.

That's pretty much it.

Were it not so sad, it would be laughable to hear leaders in the legislature fiercely arguing the pros and cons of right-to-work vs. mandatory union membership in a region that has and will have no jobs regardless of either option.

The problem in this region of West Virginia isn't right to work or unions — states all across the nation are flourishing under both systems. The greatest ill keeping new jobs from being created in Southern West Virginia is that it's simply not accessible.

Have you ever tried to get to Welch from the industrial hub of Wytheville, Virginia, which, as the crow flies, is only 42 miles away? It's a heck of an all-day road trip. Tight turns, massive hills, and 25 mph speed traps that seem to prey on out of state tags.

And the same thing can be said for much of the counties of Wyoming,

Photos: Abandonded storefronts in Iaegar, W.Va. in 2014, courtesy Magnolia677

Mingo, and Boone.

Regardless of what one's opinion about coal is, the reality is this: It won't last forever and whether it will last into the next decade seems more questionable with each day. So what are we left to do?

IF we're smart, rather than kick and scream and yell and holler "woe is me", we'll do what all the successful economies that have survived the death of their staple industry have done: We'll start preparing for the future and be receptive to change... Something we haven't been very good at doing in Appalachia from the first moment our ancestors topped the Blue Ridge — and as a result, our children are paying immensely for our stubbornness.

So what is our future? What is the hope for our economies in the post-coal era?

As a travel writer for a travel website, it feels weird to say this, but tourism is not our future.

Being the home of the Hatfield–McCoy saga is great, but if you think that's going to be our salvation, you're crazier than they were... and let's not kid ourselves, these people weren't heroes, they were crazies.

Yes, ATV trails have done wonders for a handful of restaurants and tiny inns and a couple of four-wheeler shops, but if any person thinks that being the four-wheeler capital of the world is going to put food on thousands of tables across Southern West Virginia, they're sorely mistaken.

We must aim for something higher than being another Gatlinburg or Orlando. Because the dirty truth that no one seems to enjoy mentioning about these types of economies is that they make a small percentage of folks on the very top super rich and everyone else finds themselves cleaning hotel rooms or taking tickets for minimum wage.

If the leaders in the state legislature want Southern West Virginia to be competitive in the decades to come, they must make our region attractive to manufacturers. Thanks to generations of boys and girls having spent countless hours in grandpa's garage, fixing what most others would have thrown away years earlier, we have a population that is ready and capable of producing anything imaginable — the only problem is there is no road capable of bringing in large quantities of raw materials or exporting finished products.

Fortunately, we don't have to reinvent the wheel when it comes to finding a solution to this problem.

Twenty years ago, the Federal government began moving forward with a plan to construct Interstate-73, a highway that would link Myrtle Beach, South Carolina, to Michigan, and the route would follow the pathway of US-52 through West Virginia — right through the heart of the most economically devastated counties in America.

Sadly, outside of the State of North Carolina, little has been done in two decades in order to move this project forward.

West Virginia has done some intermittent work in patches along US-52, but frankly considering the fact that this country put a man on the moon in less than a decade after setting its mind to do so (with less technology than most calculators have today), the work that has been done over twenty years time would be laughable… were it not so serious.

Appalachian Magazine recently had the opportunity to speak with West Virginia Senator Greg Boso, who is the chairman of the Senate's Transportation Committee.

A civil engineer, Boso is familiar with the project and had this to say, "I recognize that the I-73/I-74 corridor is an important piece of transportation infrastructure and hasn't received its due. This corridor will open up the expanse of southern WV as it provides connectivity between key urban and metropolitan centers with tourism opportunities."

Boso said that the project could be funded through a public-private partnership arrangement or through a publicly sponsored bonding project with debt service retired through tolling, much as was previously accomplished on the WV Turnpike.

"What we will be doing is taking several pieces of legislation that have been presented and formulating a study resolution that, during the next year, we'll work cooperatively with the WV Department of Transportation to reasonably understand the impact to the local communities and the opportunity to be successful with projected traffic," said the senator, adding, "We'll rely on the assistance of the DOT to help find additional industries that may be utilized to aid in the expansion process that would bring economic development to the southern region of West Virginia."

Though studies, funding debates and final construction on projects such as these often take years, even decades, each day that passes leaves West Virginia's population 27 individuals lower, three of whom died from overdoses.

If this legislature, governor and President do anything over the next four years, may it be that they made the most devastated region of the nation accessible and once and for all freed up our economy to do more than mine coal or sell Hatfield & McCoy t-shirts.

The Underground Coal Fire That's Been Burning for 53 Years

Appalachian Magazine Staff

Not too long ago, the West Virginia Division of Forestry warned residents of the Mountain State that "Underground coal seams can catch fire and burn for years. Flames from these fires often make their way to the surface and start wildfires."

If there is any doubt concerning the validity of the governmental agency's warning, one simply needs to travel to the state's northern neighbor, Pennsylvania, to see firsthand the havoc an underground coal fire can cause for those living topside.

On May 27, 1962, a fire was ignited that eventually reached an underground seam of coal in the central-Pennsylvania borough of Centralia.

It is believed that the fire was started deliberately under the direction of the local town council as part of a clean-up effort aimed at ridding the community of an illegal dumping site near the entrance of an abandoned strip mine. The fire unintentionally ignited a seam of coal, however, and an underground fire was started that continues to burn to this day – more than 53 years later.

Today, the conflagration (roughly one-hundred yards underneath the Keystone State's topsoil) has expanded to include an eight-mile stretch of 3,700 acres of underground coal.

Perhaps even more shocking than the fact that a fire has been burning in Pennsylvania for over a half-century is the fact that scientists estimate that the underground blaze will continue to burn for another 250 years.

Sadly, the fire which was lit in order to make the community more attractive is responsible for turning the borough into a virtual ghost town.

In 1980, over 1,000 people lived in the village, today, only seven individuals remain, making the town Pennsylvania's least populated borough and one of America's least populated localities.

By the summer of 1962, townspeople began to complain about foul odors leaking from the mine site.

An investigation confirmed what everyone feared – there was indeed a smoldering and out of control fire underneath the ground.

From here, the narrative becomes muddy and somewhat controversial. It is alleged that the town council sent a letter to the Lehigh Valley Coal Company as formal notice of the fire. The council is reported to have decided to hide the true origin of the fire out of a fear that by admitting to having started the blaze, the community would most likely not receive any help from the company.

By August, state mine inspectors found that the underground fire had created lethal levels of carbon monoxide. The findings forced all mines in the mining town to close

In the weeks ahead, tens of thousands of cubic square yards of dirt were excavated in an effort to contain the blaze, sadly, all of the efforts proved to be in vain.

In 1963, the Commonwealth of Pennsylvania dedicated over a half-million dollars toward containing the fire; however, the state abandoned its bold project to entrench the fire after three attempts proved unsuccessful and far more costly than expected.

Over the next decade and a half, the underground fire continued to burn as unsuspecting townspeople walked above the soil.

The problem was again realized in 1979, when a gas station owner inserted a dipstick into one of his underground tanks to check the fuel level and it came out hot. He lowered a thermometer on a string and was shocked to discover that the temperature of the gasoline in the tank was 172 °F.

The following year, residents of the community began reporting adverse health effects from the byproducts of the fire: carbon monoxide, carbon dioxide, and low oxygen levels.

In 1981, a 12-year-old boy named Todd Domboski was playing in his backyard when a 4 ft. wide, 150 ft. deep, sinkhole opened beneath his feet. Clinging to a tree root, the boy held on for dear life while his 14-year-old cousin, Eric Wolfgang, saved his life by pulling him from the hole which was billowing hot steam containing lethal levels of carbon monoxide.

Describing the fire in his 1986 publication, Unseen Danger: A Tragedy of People, Government, and the Centralia Mine Fire, David DeKok wrote, "This was a world where no human could live, hotter than the planet Mercury, its atmosphere as poisonous as Saturn's. At the heart of the fire, temperatures easily exceeded 1,000 degrees Fahrenheit. Lethal clouds of carbon monoxide and other gases swirled through the rock chambers.

In just a handful of years, the town's population dropped from +1,000 (1980) to 63 (1990), to 21 (2000) to 10 (2010).

In 1984, Congress allocated more than $42 million for relocation efforts of the townspeople. Most of the residents accepted buyout offers from the Federal government and moved to the nearby communities of Mount Carmel and Ashland. A few families opted to stay despite urgings against doing so from Pennsylvania officials.

In 1992, Pennsylvania governor Bob Casey invoked eminent domain on all properties in the borough, condemning all the buildings within. A subsequent legal effort by residents to have the decision reversed failed.

In 2002, the U.S. Postal Service revoked Centralia's ZIP code, 17927, and in 2009, the Commonwealth began formally evicting the remaining residents of Centralia.

By July 2012, the last remaining holdouts of the community once known as Centralia lost their final appeal and were again ordered to leave. State and local officials, however, reached an agreement with the seven remaining residents on October 29, 2013, allowing them to live out their lives in Centralia, after which the rights of their properties will be taken through eminent domain.

Today, the half-century old underground coal fire of Centralia serves as a reminder to the nation of the delicate balance that is life on earth.

The Georgia County Excluded
From the State's Quarter
Appalachian Magazine Staff

Secluded in the extreme northwestern section of the State of Georgia reside the independent and free spirited people of Dade County.

Unlike much of the state, Dade County is positioned in the Appalachian Mountains and boasts of breathtaking mountain vistas including the 1,800' deep Cloudland Canyon – complete with two waterfalls cascading into pools below.

Since the county's formation in 1837, the people of this rugged land were forced to adopt a self-reliant attitude. Separated from the rest of their state by a massive canyon, the State of Georgia did not have a road connecting to Dade County until 1939. Prior to that time, the county could only be accessed through Alabama and Tennessee.

Feeling forgotten by state officials in Atlanta, county leaders seized the opportunity to make a clean break from the state during the onset of the Civil War.

Robin Ford, a local reporter, described the county's secession in the following words:

"Dade County, sick and tard of Georgia's shillyin' and shallyin' at the beginning of the Civil War, seceded individually from the Union in 1860, declaring its independence not only from the U.S. but from a state that couldn't make up its mind. Thus the feisty little county was a sovereign nation – the Independent State of Dade..."

Unlike the rest of the southern states that seceded from the union in the opening days of the Lincoln Administration, union officials overlooked forcing Dade County to officially rejoin the union, following the war. A tiny detail that was not overlooked by county residents, who continued to claim sovereignty over the next 85 years.

It wasn't until the end of World War II – in a frenzy of patriotism – that the county chose to once again officially pledge allegiance to the United States. On July 4, 1945, a telegram from President Harry S Truman was read at a celebration marking the county's rejoining the Union.

According to Ford, "There was a military band playing, a crowd of an estimated 4,000 in front of the Dade County courthouse thunderously voting 'aye' to rejoin the U.S., a national radio broadcast and a triumphantly waved telegram from President Harry S. Truman congratulating the tiny nation of Dade on its reentry into the Union. 'Welcome home, pilgrims,' concluded Truman's message."

So for the next half-century all seemed good... until the State of Georgia's official state quarter was released on July 19, 1999.

Residents of the forgotten county immediately noticed that the state's northwestern boundary curved inward, just east of the northwesternmost county of Dade.

State leaders, as well as the federal mint, maintained that the county had been accidentally left off the quarter; though many residents of the historic community claim it was no accident – suggesting they were excluded intentionally.

Dade County Commissioner Robert Goff told *Appalachian Magazine*, "Few people know about the quarter it seems. If I mention it folks usually laugh if they are from another part of the state. I carry one to show them and when they see it's for real they ask why. I just tell them that Atlanta doesn't know we exist so they didn't know where to put us."

We asked Mr. Goff what made his county so special and his description of the place he calls home makes a person want to pack up the truck and move to northeast Georgia.

"As for special, we are a triangle shaped county. Two mountains and a valley running its length. Many people traveling through notice and remark how beautiful it is, and of course we whole heartedly agree. We are a close knit county and in times of tragedy everyone comes together like one big family."

The Dying Family Cemetery

Appalachian Magazine Staff

As a child, my world was one spent somewhere between two medians – the mountainous and free spirited hills of Southern West Virginia's coalfields and industrial Virginia.

Though I attended school in the Old Dominion, most of the life lessons I learned growing up occurred within the jagged borders of the Mountain State – it was there that I learned the value of family, heritage and the story of my ancestors. These traits grew to become defining principles I hope to not only exude in my own life, but to also pass down to my children.

To put it simply, West Virginians are different and proud of it. They live differently, love differently and remember differently. They... We... cherish our state's remarkable and turbulent history. We were taught to appreciate the strength of our elders and grew to treasure the stories of bloody mine wars, early settlers and grandma's pappy. In West Virginia, history lives through the impoverished children who sat at their daddy's feet, listening to stories of brave men and women who gladly laid down their lives for the principle of a matter. Most early miners had nothing to leave to their children, nothing except for hundreds of stories and thousands of memories; yet these were the best inheritances any child could ever hope to receive.

It should then seem as no surprise that when it comes to disposing of our dead, we, in the hills of West Virginia, do things far differently than most other Americans. While the rest of the nation, by and large, lower their grandfathers beneath the dirt in a public cemetery – surrounded by hundreds or even thousands of strangers – West Virginians often return their fathers to plats of land that have been in the family's name for countless decades or even centuries.

There, the very land of the family cemetery is sacred. For many, the thought of being buried anywhere other than alongside their brothers, parents, grandparents and even earlier generations would be unacceptable.

Just outside of the town limits of the community of Delbarton, in Mingo County, my family has a consecrated piece of ground that has been the site of countless tears, yet holds a dear place in the hearts of all of us who share a common name and common heritage – it is the Farley Family Cemetery. It's not the only family cemetery alongside the winding stream known as Elk Creek – in fact there are a countless number of family burial sites throughout the valley, but this one is ours.

It is the only site I have ever seen my strong and unwavering father shed tears. It is the only site where I can come within a few feet of my great-great-great grandfather. It is the most sacred spot in the world for our family, yet it is one of thousands of family cemeteries in West Virginia; all of which are just as dear to someone else.

As the Virginia pioneers pushed farther west, they encountered a world that was isolated, rugged and a place where death's cold shadow lurked behind every passing turn. Times were hard, but these men and women were resilient and they pressed on – undeterred by the sting of death.

As a matter of practicality, during the early years of Western Virginia's history, families would clear out a small plot of land, often in wooded areas bordering their fields, and bury a child that succumbed to a fever or cough. Next, an uncle would be buried along side the child. Then a second child would be buried, followed by mother and father.

For the surviving children, these hallowed acres was the site of pain, maturity and the reality that life is indeed fragile — to put it simply, that piece of ground made them.

Therefore, as they grew older, they cherished those old burial sites, painstakingly mowing the sites, managing additional plots and working to ensure their children were grossly aware of the story each of the cold headstones told.

The remnants of these ancient cemeteries are still visible today, often just a few yards from the old family home place.

For our family, like so many others, the family cemetery remains a critical component of who we are and each time a family member dies, there is never a question relating to where that person will be buried.

Sadly, those old men who dedicated so many hours to maintaining the gardens of the dead — many of which have graves marked only by concrete (marble was too costly for many early West Virginians), have now joined their mothers and fathers beneath the soil in those same hallowed resting places.

With their passing, the question remains, "Who's going to fill their shoes?" Who will step in and continue the work that had been passed down to them? Who in the 21st century even has time to do this?

These are very good questions and as the writer drives through the state and sees so many grave sites and family cemeteries grown over, he can't help but answer, "very few."

The West Virginia Town
That Applied For Soviet Foreign Aid
Appalachian Magazine Staff

Wedged between a towering horseshoe-shaped mountain to its north, east and south, the tiny community of Vulcan, West Virginia's western edge is flanked by the murky waters of the Tug River — one of America's most storied waterways. The hamlet's geography, decided eons ago, leaves it entirely ostracized from its neighbors and were it not for the discovery of coal in the general vicinity of the land, a great case could be made that the area would never have been inhabited.

However, coal was discovered in the region in the opening days of the Twentieth Century and soon, a mining camp grew up in what would become a map dot known as Vulcan, West Virginia.

The coal camp eventually grew into a thriving community and the area became home to a countess number of individuals who found steady work and acceptable wages in nearby coal mines.

Unfortunately, by the early 1960s the mines, which served as the small town's lifeblood, dried up – causing all operations to cease.

Soon, what was once a flourishing hamlet had been reduced to little more than twenty families; all of which were remaining holdouts who refused to leave the place they now knew as home.

Describing Vulcan, West Virginia, in his 1972 book, They'll Cut Off Your Project, Huey Perry wrote, "Their biggest problem was that the state had forgotten to build a road into the community. Although state maps showed a road into Vulcan, it was nowhere to be found. The only way people could get in and out was to drive up the Kentucky side and walk across a swinging bridge, which was too narrow for a vehicle. The bridge had been built by the coal company years before and was on the verge of collapse; although there were boards missing, the children had to walk across it to catch the school bus on the Kentucky side..."

The grievances held by local residents was not limited to state and county officials. According to Perry, the children of Vulcan, at times, were forced to crawl under parked railroad coal cars on their way to school. The track, which ran parallel with the river, blocked access to the swinging bridge – the town's only legal egress – leaving school children with no other choice but to crawl under the parked train cars.

One of the former school children who grew up in Vulcan, Troy Blankenship, even lost part of his left leg when he was eleven, crawling under a coal car that was parked.

Further angering the townspeople was an N & W Railroad side road that ran adjacent to the main line of the tracks, which passed through

Vulcan. The road ran to the nearby community of Delmore, approximately five miles to the north of Vulcan; however, the company locked the entrances to the road on both ends, hanging a "No Trespassing" sign. Those caught trespassing by using the road were prosecuted and fined.

The railroad company defended their actions by saying that the road was too dangerous for civilian vehicles, arguing that opening up the road to residents would "jeopardize the railroad, and the railroad would be responsible if an accident occurred."

Norfolk and Western maintained that the problem was a local problem and that they were not responsible for providing transportation in and out of the impoverished community.

Despite repeated attempts to convince government leaders to repair their bridge, no action was ever taken and over the next decade, conditions deteriorated significantly. According to reports, the failing bridge eventually collapsed in 1975, leaving the residents of Vulcan hemmed between the Tug Fork to their west and impassable mountains to their east.

Residents then began illegally using the railroad owned gravel road, which, at times, proved to be hazardous.

Still, West Virginia officials were reluctant to rebuild the collapsed bridge, citing a lack of traffic and cost, as opposed to other needs of the state.

The election of Governor Jay Rockefeller wrought little change for the economies of southern West Virginia, leaving many residents in the Mountain State's coalfield region to allege that their localities were not receiving a fair amount of money from the state's coffers.

Soon a popular bumper sticker began appearing on vehicles throughout the coalfield-region, stating, "These roads could Rock-a-Feller!"

Feeling forsaken by their own government, after repeated pleas to have a new bridge constructed, the people of this West Virginia community made an unprecedented move which soon garnered international headlines. At the height of the Cold War, residents of Vulcan wrote to the Soviet Embassy in Washington, as well as to communist officials in East Germany, detailing their plight and requesting foreign aid from the nations.

Sensing an opportunity to shame the American government, the Kremlin immediately dispatched journalists to the United States.

Interviewing the residents of Vulcan and broadcasting their troubles to the rest of the world, the government in Moscow did what the residents of Vulcan had been attempting to do for years, bring attention to their transportation nightmare.

By mid-December 1977, newspaper headlines around the country were announcing, "Small Town Seeks Russ Foreign Aid" (Spokane Daily Chronicle).

The Spokane Daily Chronicle wrote, "Soviet officials were amused today by reports that the small town of Vulcan, W.Va. has appealed to the Kremlin for foreign aid... The town, with a population of 200, asked the Soviet government for financial help to build a bridge after the town was turned down by the U.S. and West Virginia governments."

Local radio stations began reporting bomb threats toward any bridge built with communist help.

Embarrassed by the attention their lack of assistance was receiving, state officials wasted no time in committing $1.3 million and built a bridge for the tiny community.

Though the only legal way to access the community of Vulcan, West Virginia, continues to be via Pike County, Kentucky, residents of the former mining town now enjoy a one-lane graffiti covered bridge connecting them to the 'outside world!'

Useless Appalachian "Bathroom Reading"

Why We No Longer Have Silver Quarters
Appalachian Magazine Staff

As an amateur coin collector, it pains me to divulge this information to thousands of my fellow countrymen, but it's time you stop throwing away real silver as if it were only worth 25¢!

If you've been around for any length of time at all, you'll agree that they just don't make stuff like they once did not too long ago. Whether it's heavy machinery, cookware, children's toys or something as insignificant as a screwdriver, there's no denying that in the vast majority of cases, the things we leave with out of a store in modern day America are of far less quality than was the case a half-century ago – and unfortunately, this literally includes the change in our pockets.

As some of the folks who have been around for a while will testify, coinage just doesn't feel like it used to.

This is because back in the "good o'le days", US coins, including the quarter dollar coin were minted from silver – in order to pass the mint's strict quality control guidelines, all quarters between 1932-1964 had to be comprised of 90% silver, equating to approximately 0.18084 troy ounces of pure silver.

Unfortunately, the year of 1964 presented a severe shortage of U.S. coins, particularly for quarters and dimes. This was due to the fact that the American public had begun hoarding silver coins in the face of escalating silver prices.

Banks across the nation began holding "green sales", exchanging $1 bills for 98¢ worth of coins. On the street, silver coins were going for an even greater amount.

On July 30, 1964, The Delaware County Times, reported, "Coin grabbers are selling rolls of new dimes worth $5 for $7.50 and rolls of new Kennedy 50¢ pieces worth $10 for $11.50 to $17. In at least once instance a single new 50¢ piece coin sold for $15."

Assistant Treasury Secretary Robert Wallace, stated, "Nothing short of a crash program will solve the problem," adding, "We are now taking drastic measures."

Those drastic measures culminated the following year with the passage of The Coinage Act of 1965, which eliminated silver from the circulating United States dime and quarter dollar coins. It also reduced the silver content of the half dollar from 90 percent to 40 percent; silver in the half dollar was subsequently eliminated by a 1970 law.

Basically, by making the nation's coins worthless was the only way the Federal government could prod people back into spending them again!

Today's quarters are copper-nickel clad, with a layer of pure copper in the center. One of the most noticeable differences of modern quarters is the ringing sound they make when dropped onto a hard surface, as compared to the flat "thump" silver quarters make.

So here's a very basic and simple rule of thumb to keep in mind when looking at your change: if you come across a quarter or dime struck from 1964 or in previous years, you're holding an extinct coin comprised of approximately 0.18084 troy ounces of pure silver.

With silver prices currently at $17.27 per ounce, that makes pre-1965 quarters worth roughly $3.12 in their metal alone… That's 12.5 times their face value. Now you can see why folks were hoarding these things… as well as why you should be kicking yourself for not taking the time to inspect all those quarters you've been mindlessly dropping into vending machines over the past four decades!

Technically, Russia & Japan are still at War...
In World War II
Appalachian Magazine Staff

Though the United States and Japan formally ended hostilities with the signing of the Japanese Instrument of Surrender aboard the deck of the USS Missouri on September 2, 1945, the Japanese government and military never signed such a document with the former Soviet Union at the close of the conflict – instead, the two sides merely ceased fighting each other without any formal declaration.

Nearly 71 years later, a state of war still quietly exists between the Tokyo government and her World War II adversary in Moscow.

If you believe that this is a mere technicality, think again, as a 2012 Pew Global Attitudes Project survey revealed that 72% of Japanese people view Russia unfavorably, making Japan the country with the most anti-Russian sentiment surveyed.

The reason the two sides never got around to signing a formal peace treaty was due to the fact that the two nations could not reach an agreement pertaining to the Kuril Islands, a chain of Russian-occupied islands which Japan refers to as its Northern Territories.

Approximately 20,000 inhabit these islands today, the majority of which are ethnic Russians and Ukrainians.

In an attempt to discourage any Japanese invasion of the islands, Russia has permanently manned several villages with soldiers as well as placed a significant number of its elite Border Guard Service troops and Russian Federation police in key villages along the island chain.

In an effort to officially put an end to World War II, the most devastating war in Japanese history, the country's prime minister, Shinzo Abe, recently stated that he was open to signing a peace treaty with Moscow.

According to the BBC, Abe "told reporters that both leaders recognized that the lack of such a document for 70 years was 'abnormal.'"

Since taking office in 2012 the prime minister has tried to improve relations with Moscow.

How a Disabled Truck Transformed a Polluted West Virginia Creek into a Popular Fishing Hole

Appalachian Magazine Staff

Unfortunately, it's not too uncommon to hear of a disabled truck polluting a stream and killing off a countless number of fish in the process; however, in the early-1970s, a disabled truck was responsible for transforming a polluted West Virginia stream into what would become a thriving waterway for trout.

A half-century ago, West Virginia's Elkhorn Creek in the state's southern coalfields had garnered a reputation as being one of the most polluted waterways in the entire Appalachian region. Used in the nasty job of washing coal, the overwhelming majority of locals viewed the tainted creek as being an eyesore and a scourge upon the landscape of Mercer and McDowell counties — thus the creek was used as a sewer collection system for many years and the thought of fishing in the stream was completely out of the question, as raw sewer and trash seemed to be the only thing one could find in the Ohio River bound creek.

Amazingly, all of this changed in the 1970s — by sheer accident.

As the story goes, a hatchery truck heavy laden with live Rainbow Trout was en route to a river when it broke down while traveling along US-52.

Fearing the fish would die if left in the stagnating water of the broke down truck, the driver unilaterally made a decision that would reshape communities for years to come: he released his entire payload into the polluted Elkhorn Creek. Though there wasn't much hope for the fish to live in the dirty water below the roadway, the slim-to-none chances were better than if they'd stayed in the baking water.

In the initial years that followed, this stocking of Rainbow Trout went unnoticed to most, until dozens of local residents began reporting the presence of very large Rainbow Trout in what was believed to have been a dead waterway.

Turns out, the water supplying much of the creek is emitted from old coalmines, making it consistently cold throughout the year, allowing the trout an opportunity to spawn naturally. Additionally, the coal in eastern McDowell County is relatively low in sulfur, therefore its effects upon the fish is minimal.

The discoveries led the West Virginia Division of Natural Resources to introduce Brown Trout into the Elkhorn in what proved to be a successful program in 1993.

Today, the Elkhorn Creek has become a cherished waterway in many of the communities through which it flows, with businesses catering to anglers wishing to take advantage of one of the very places in West Virginia rainbow and brown trout spawn naturally.

Sadly, the clean up effort still has a long ways to go, as trash often lines the banks and waterway of the Elkhorn. "Abandoned homes, many of them crumbling and hollowed-out shells, commonly line the stream banks, testaments to better times or at least different ones when King Coal ruled," writes Game & Fish Magazine.

Numerous organizations and individuals, however, have made it their mission to clean up this incredible West Virginia creek and with growing national interest in fishing the unique waterway that seems tailor made for the largescale production of trout, naturally, the outlook for this historic waterway is bright.

Due to the fact that the creek is not stocked and the trout spawn naturally, fishermen are urged to practice catch and release while fishing in the stream.

The United States' Secret Plan to Invade Canada

Appalachian Magazine Staff

Today, most Americans see our friendly neighbors to the north as being nothing more than distant relatives we get to see every holiday... we typically run into them somewhere on a four-lane highway behind the wheel of a snowbird mobile.

Canada is our country's biggest trading partner, fellow ally against the "axis of evil" and has proven herself as a reliable friend time and time again.

Oddly enough, this intracontinental friendship is a relatively new undertaking – for centuries the two governments viewed each other with an incredible level of distrust and downright disdain.

The woes can be traced back to the early days of the Revolutionary War. While the lower thirteen American colonies were in open rebellion to the British Crown, the settlements in what is now Canada proved loyal to the London government, rejecting America's sovereignty and even going to war against the Continental Army.

This faithfulness to the Crown would eventually lead to dozens of military engagements between the citizens of the two governments, including an unsuccessful American siege on Quebec in 1775, as well as a failed attempt to conquer the British dependent during the War of 1812.

Though the two Anglican nations eventually learned to cohabitate on the 9.5 million square mile continent, to say they immediately became the best of friends would illustrate a gross ignorance of the turbulent relationship between the Bald Eagle and the maple leaf.

Even following a joint engagement against imperial Germany during World War I, the United States and British Canada were still extraordinarily distrusting of one another – and for good reason.

In 1974, the United States Defense Department declassified documents from the 1930s that revealed that the United States Army and Navy were devising plans to invade Canada. The plan was known as War Plan Red and was devised out of a fear that war with England, Canada's protectorate, was inevitable following World War I – turns out England owed the United States, her wartime ally, an incredible amount of money following the Great War and the two nations were in bitter disagreement regarding the terms of payback.

Now before you get too upset with the United States, you should also know that immediately following World War I, nearly a decade before the American plan was hatched, Canada went to work devising its own plan to invade the United States: Defence Scheme No. 1.

In 1921 Canadian plan called for a surprise invasion of the northern United States should relations between the two governments continue to worsen.

In preparing its plan to invade the United States, Canada maintained secret agents in the United States for five years

Historian Pierre Berton noted in his book Marching as to War, the investigation had "a zany flavour about it, reminiscent of the silent comedies of the day." To illustrate this, Berton quoted from the agent's reports, in which they recorded, among other things, that in Burlington, Vermont, the people were "affable" and thus unusual for Americans; that Americans drink significantly less alcohol than Canadians (this was during Prohibition). After carefully studying the people of Burlington, Vermont, the Canadian agents concluded that the people of Vermont would be serious soldiers only "if aroused" and that many Americans might be sympathetic to the British cause.

The American plan to invade Canada, put together nearly a decade later, was slightly more serious.

According to the Yankee study, a British invasion into America was likely and in such an event, English forces would use Canada as a staging ground prior to any land invasion of the United States.

In order to take away their staging ground, the report recommended a preemptive and lightning-fast invasion into Canada, occupying and / or destroying Canada's infrastructure, leaving the ports and airbases unusable to British forces.

Central to this plan was a joint US army-navy attack to capture the port city of Halifax, cutting off the Canadians from their British allies. The next objective would be to "seize Canadian Power Plants near Niagara Falls" This was to be followed by a full-scale invasion on three fronts: From Vermont to take Montreal and Quebec, from North Dakota to take over the railhead at Winnipeg, and from the Midwest to capture the strategic nickel mines of Ontario. In parallel, the U.S. Navy was to seize the Great Lakes and blockade Canada's Atlantic and Pacific ports.

Fortunately, the savior of American-Canadian relations was none other than one of the most evil men to ever walk the face of the globe, Adolph Hitler.

By the end of the decade, Hitler's Nazi Germany had begun its tyrannical conquering of Europe and Britain soon found itself in the fight of its life against Germany, as well as needing her American "allies" more than ever.

Thanks to World War II, the Cold War and cooler heads prevailing, the American-Canadian border is the longest international boundary on the planet – the vast majority of which is completely unguarded.

So the next time you see those Ontario plates cruising down the Interstate highway, just keep in mind that it is because of a man named Adolph Hitler that the United States and Canada are BFFs!

The Rattlesnake: America's First National Symbol

Appalachian Magazine Staff

Few species embody the American Spirit quite as well as the Bald Eagle.

Over the past two centuries, this majestic bird's likeness has stormed the beaches of Normandy, seen combat against Barbary pirates and even landed on the moon.

With its magnificent image gracing everything from our currency to the rug in the Oval Office, it's hard to imagine any other animal serving as the symbol of our Grand Republic – but as hard as it may be to imagine, when it comes to national symbols, the Bald Eagle showed up to the party a little late.

Long before the soaring eagle was stamped onto the side of fighter jets refueling over Afghanistan, the eastern diamondback and timber rattlesnakes were enjoying their time in the sun, personifying what it meant to be American.

When the early colonists arrived in the New World, one of the first creatures to greet them was the eastern diamondback rattlesnake. Coming from a land where the only poisonous snake was the extremely passive Adder, the British settlers were terrified by the rattlesnake, whose bites often equated to certain death among 17th century colonists.

Evidence of the incredible fear early English settlers felt toward the native snakes can be spotted in the dozens of newspapers articles from the period which offer almost laughable instructions on how to survive a bite from the ferocious rattlesnake.

By the mid-1700s, however, Americans had come to realize that the continent had been inhabited by these poisonous serpents long before they had arrived and accepted their presence as a mere fact of life in the New World. Around this same time, the nation began experiencing a rise in tensions with the Motherland.

In 1750, the Crown began sending convicted criminals to live in America, an act that outraged colonists who had no desire to live alongside thieves and revilers.

The following year, a satirical commentary published in his Pennsylvania Gazette, by legendary writer Ben Franklin suggested that in response, colonists begin sending rattlesnakes to England.

Franklin's popular article made him famous and gave the American colonists a newfound pride in the crawling reptile that had for so long haunted their dreams.

A handful of years later, Franklin again published a cartoon featuring the rattlesnake, this time under the banner, "Join or Die." His famous woodcut presented a snake cut into eight sections. It represented the colonies, with New England joined together as the head and South Carolina as the tail, following their order along the coast. This was the first political cartoon published in an American newspaper.

In the days ahead, the American colonies came to identify more with their own communities and the concept of liberty, rather than as subjects of an international British Empire.

As a result, the people of the soon-to-be independent nation began to actively seek out icons that were unique to the Americas. The rattlesnake, like the bald eagle and American Indian, came to symbolize American ideas and society.

As the American Revolution picked up steam, the snake began to see more use as a beloved symbol of the colonies. In 1774, Paul Revere added Franklin's iconic cartoon to the nameplate of his paper, the Massachusetts Spy. Atop the header of Revere's paper, the rattlesnake was fighting a British dragon.

In December 1775, Benjamin Franklin published an essay in the Pennsylvania Journal under the pseudonym American Guesser in which he suggested that the rattlesnake was a good symbol for the American spirit:

"I recollected that her eye excelled in brightness, that of any other animal, and that she has no eye-lids—She may therefore be esteemed an emblem of vigilance.—She never begins an attack, nor, when once engaged, ever surrenders: She is therefore an emblem of magnanimity and true courage.—As if anxious to prevent all pretensions of quarreling with her, the weapons with which nature has furnished her, she conceals in the roof of her mouth, so that, to those who are unacquainted with her, she appears to be a most defenseless animal; and even when those weapons are shown and extended for her defense, they appear weak and contemptible; but their wounds however small, are decisive and fatal:— Conscious of this, she never wounds till she has generously given notice, even to her enemy, and cautioned him against the danger of stepping on her.—Was I wrong, Sir, in thinking this a strong picture of the temper and conduct of America?"

That same year, the rattlesnake found its way onto one of the first American flags, the bright yellow Gadsen Flag, over the words, "Don't Tread on Me."

Roughly a year and a half later, the rattlesnake was officially adopted by the Continental Congress to serve as the nation's first symbol, approving the design for the official Seal of the War Office. Today, the rattlesnake is still included in the design of the Department tge Army's official seal – having served continuously for over 236 years.

The Flu Pandemic That Gave West Virginia "Robert Byrd"

Appalachian Magazine Staff

Driving through West Virginia, it doesn't take very long to realize that a man named Robert C. Byrd made an impact on the Mountain State. Just about every county has a road, bridge, school, community center, or all of the above named in his honor.

The state's beloved senator served the people of the mountains from 1959 until his death in June 2010.

Described by Republican and Democratic counterparts alike as being a true American statesmen, Byrd championed the legislative branch of government and often frustrated political opponents with his encyclopedic knowledge of the inner workings of the United States Senate.

At the time of his death, Byrd was the only serving U.S. Senator who had voted to authorize a new state entrance into the Union.

In eulogy, the Speaker of the House stated, "Throughout his historic career in the House and Senate, he never stopped working to improve the lives of the people of West Virginia."

That may be true, but in reality, Robert C. Byrd was neither a West Virginian nor "Robert C. Byrd" at the time of his birth.

Born on November 20, 1917, in North Wilkesboro, North Carolina, "Robert Byrd" was actually named Cornelius Calvin Sale, Jr. His parents, Cornelius Calvin Sale, Sr. and Ada Mae Kirby Sale, were lifelong residents of the Carolina County of Wilkes, a rural farming community that rests in the foothills of the Blue Ridge Mountains.

Sadly for the young family, a deadly pandemic of the H1N1 influenza virus infected roughly half a billion of the world's population and Ada Mae Kirby Sale was no exception.

The 1918 flu pandemic presented an unusually deadly string, which in addition to infecting the major population centers of the world, reached remote parts of the Pacific islands and the extreme northern Arctic, killing between 50 to 100 million individuals — roughly five percent of the world's population. The pandemic has been described as one of the deadliest natural disasters in human history.

Growing sicker and reading the daily news reports describing the ever increasing number of H1N1 deaths, Ada Sale requested that her children be dispersed among relatives in the event of her death.

Just ten days prior to her infant son's first birthday, Ada died, leaving her husband a widower and her children motherless.

In honor of her wishes, the children were separated and given to relatives, the youngest, Cornelius Sale, Jr., was given to an aunt and uncle who lived in a Raleigh County, West Virginia, community just south of Beckley.

Cornelius was soon adopted by his uncle and aunt, Titus and Vlurma Byrd, who changed his name to Robert Carlyle Byrd and raised him to appreciate the Mountain State, its people, rich history and music.

Byrd would graduate valedictorian at Mark Twain High School in Tams, West Virginia, and successively attended Beckley College, Concord College, Morris Harvey College, and Marshall University, all in West Virginia.

Regardless of one's political views, it is impossible to doubt the fact that West Virginia is at the epicenter of Byrd's legacy. It is also difficult to imagine what present-day West Virginia or America would look like, had a deadly string of the H1N1 Virus never infected a poor mother in Wilkes County, North Carolina.

Beyond
Our Mountains

Christopher Columbus' "Message in a Bottle" Could Still be Floating Aimlessly Somewhere on Earth

Appalachian Magazine Staff

Somewhere in the vast expanse of our planet's ocean may be a floating barrel that is worth more than its weight in gold. The only problem is that there are approximately 139.7 million square miles of ocean and the tiny cask is probably no larger than a couple of square feet at the very most — further compounding the hunt is the fact that thanks to 500 years of ocean currents, the barrel could be anywhere by now, if it's even still in existence.

The story dates back to the late-1400s, aboard the ship of a famous explorer of whom you undoubtedly learned as a child. Remember, "Columbus sailed the ocean blue in fourteen hundred and ninety-two."

Turns out, upon returning from his newly discovered world, our boy Christopher got fearful that God was going to kill him (sounds like the man had an unclean conscience, but that's another story!), in which case, the world would never learn of his incredible discovery, thereby robbing him of becoming immortally celebrated.

These fears were exacerbated on February 14, 1493, when the crew found themselves at the mercy of a violent North Atlantic storm.

Historian Laurence Bergreen writes, "Columbus became convinced that 'Our Lord wished him to perish.' At the same time, he reminded himself of his mission and the news of his exploits that he was bringing to Ferdinnd and Isabella. The more important the news became in his mind, the more fearful he became that he would not be able to deliver it, and that all his discoveries and sacrifices would be for naught."

In their book, The Worlds of Christopher Columbus, William & Carla Phillips detail the drastic measures Columbus took in order to preserve his legacy and ensure that the world would remember him and his discovery.

"In his desperation to claim the credit that was his due, Columbus wrote as much about the voyage as he could on a parchment addressed to Fernando and Isabel. He prepared the message secretly and then wrapped the parchment securely in a waxed cloth. Ordering a barrel brought to him, he placed the packet inside and had the barrel thrown into the sea. The crew assumed the packet and the barrel had something to do with an act of piety and were spared the alarm of knowing that the admiral doubted they would survive."

Fortunately for the members of the Crew and for Columbus himself, they did survive and the famed explorer had the opportunity to brag about the incredible land he had discovered on the far side of the globe — making him go down in history as one of the most famous individuals of the past 1,000 years.

Unfortunately, the same cannot be said about Columbus' overboard barrel, as it was never discovered — or if was, the finders exercised wisdom and kept their mouths shut.

But where it is now is anybody's guess and the world may never know the whereabouts of this incredible handwritten note sealed by Mr. Columbus himself.

Is there any chance that Columbus' lost cask is still silently sitting somewhere, just waiting to be discovered?

Surprisingly, yes. Though the odds of this are very slim and the probability of you actually being the person to find this priceless historical discovery are even lower, but yes, it's still possible.

I mean, afterall, the world's most premier militaries and nations have been searching for a massive jet liner that crashed in the ocean for years now and no ones been able to locate it and the size difference between a tiny barrel and a Malaysian airliner are incomparable — the oceans are a massive, massive, massive, body and looking for something as small as a tiny cask may be harder than finding a needle in a hay stack.

Yet, due to the fact that the interior of the barrel was lined and sealed, many scientists believe that it is quite plausible to conceive that the cask has petrified or sealed to the point that the timeless contents hidden within may have been preserved.

In fact, the +500 year old wooden cask rotting is not nearly as great of a concern as the container being sunk to the bottom thanks to the weight of the numerous marine organisms. These "marine organisms" probably attached themselves to the floating message in a bottle almost immediately upon being cast overboard, but the level of damage they may have caused by now is unknown.

The greatest hope of an individual ever finding Columbus' secret message is that the tumbling cask made it to a shoreline sometime within the first eight to ten months of being tossed to the sea. There, we can hope that erosion did its perfect work, sealing the timeless artifact beneath a sandy beach somewhere, only to be discovered at some distant date by workers preparing to lay the footers for the next big high rise condominium at a surfside resort.

Should Columbus' message ever be discovered, in would shatter the current world record for duration of message in a bottle discovery: 151 years (a Pacific Islander cast a message in a bottle into the ocean in 1784 and the note was not discovered until the eve of World War II just off the coast of Japan in 1935.

On April 17, 2015, a bottle washed upon a German shore from George Parker Bidder, an English marine biologists. The note was dated, November 30, 1906, 108 years earlier.

Is it possible that Columbus' note is still out there, just waiting to be discovered? You can bet your butt it is, but I wouldn't quit my day job to go out searching for it, though you have to admit, it would be the adventure of a lifetime!

America's Most Unique Island is Vanishing Away Just Off the Virginia Coast

Appalachian Magazine Staff

PHOTO: *Tangier Island Cemetery: courtesy of baldeaglebluff*

Few American states, if any, can compete with the Commonwealth of Virginia when it comes to geographic diversity.

Serving as America's oldest permanent settlement, the state's east coast is comprised of proud seafaring communities and is home to the world's largest naval station. Just a few hundred miles inland and you might as well be a million miles from the ocean, as the sandy beaches give way to the Blue Ridge Mountains and millions of acres of cow pastures and John Deere tractors busily making the "spring cut" of hay. Continue westward even farther and the ridge and valleys will eventually surrender to the jagged mountains of the state's coalfields in far Southwestern Virginia.

Here, at least one of the state's counties is west of Detroit, Michigan, and closer to nine state capitals than her very own in Richmond. Residents in this region of the state have far more in common with a farmer in West Texas (probably because the founders of Texas came from this region), a thousand miles away than with their fellow Virginians living in Fairfax only a couple hundred miles to their northeast — in these parts, the term "Northern Virginia" is seldom ever spoken in a positive manner and for what it's worth the feeling seems mutual in the dark blue localities around our nation's capital.

Virginia is a state that has always struggled to remain united – this was evidenced greatly during the American Civil War – and the problem hasn't gotten much better in the 150 years that have followed.

When the state legislature meets each January it becomes very evident to any onlooker that the people who call Virginia home are as different as the lands they represent and so are their accents.

The Tidwater representatives will be heard pronouncing water as "Wardor", while representatives from the Southside may be heard asking "Watch chu plan to do ah-boat tha court hoose?" While the state's Appalachian representatives may be overheard saying they "Liketa never got the young'uns in their district the funding they deserved."

Yet, as fascinating as these Virginia accents may be, they pale in comparison to the voices of the inhabitants of Virginia's Tangier Island, America's most unique and fascinating island.

Located in the Chesapeake Bay midway between the state's mainland and the Delmarva Penninsula, Tangier Island is only 1.2 square miles in size, but what makes this island so unique are the 727 individuals who call this forgotten island home.

The first white settlers arrived on the tiny island in the late-1600s and early 1700s from Southwest England. More than a dozen miles from the mainlands of Virginia or Delmarva, these individuals mostly kept to themselves, enjoying a simple and isolated life on a remote island in the Chesapeake Bay.

With no bridges or roads, the only way to reach this .86-mile x 1-mile island was by taking a +12 mile boat ride – and so the isolation of this placed continued for roughly three centuries until a small runway was constructed on the island's west coast in 1969.

Owing to this isolation, the tiny island community has attracted the attention of linguists because the 17th Century English Restoration era dialect spoken by the island's natives has been largely preserved and has remained unchanged for more than 300 years.

The words spoken by residents of the island sound more like a northern English, Scottish, or Irish accent than it does an American accent and many islanders have often been mistaken for being from the UK or Ireland when traveling to areas outside of the Chesapeake Bay. The brogue is most distinctive the further south one travels on the Outer Banks, with it being the thickest on Ocracoke Island and Harkers Island. Locally, the accent is called "Hoi Toider", in that the term "High tider" is pronounced with a distinctive "oy" in the hard "i", in common with the Westcountry dialect found in Southwest England.

Locally, the accent is called "Hoi Toider", in that the term "High tider" is pronounced with a distinctive "oy" in the hard "i", in common with the Westcountry dialect found in Southwest England.

Owing to the island's isolation, the resident's lifestyles are characterized as laid-back and "folksy." The isolation also contributes to the prevalence of Tangier disease, a recessive genetic disorder which causes high blood cholesterol that is named after the island's residents.

There is only one school on the island, with fewer than ten children in each grade. The residents were given access to cable television and Internet through a new microwave tower in spring 2010. There are phone lines on the island. Two doctors live on the island currently, but practice in Delaware.

Although the island has one power plant, it is mainly used for emergencies but is operational. Power comes in from the Eastern Shore of Virginia.

Methodism has been and remains a very strong influence on Tangier, stemming from the charismatic preaching and revival camp meetings held there in the early 1800s by Joshua Thomas, the famed "parson of the islands." Because of their ties to the Northern Methodist Church, Tangier residents did not support slavery and refused to join the rest of Virginia in seceding from the Union during the Civil War. Traditional religious values still dominate in the community, and a local ordinance prohibits the sale of alcohol. The Tangier town council blocked Warner Brothers from using the island to film the 1999 Kevin Costner film Message in a Bottle, objecting to the script's drinking, profanity, and sex. If visitors bring their own alcohol, they are advised to be discreet and not drink it in public.

Sadly, the island is quickly vanishing away.

Standing only 3 ft. above sea level, Tangier Island has always been in a very fragile position, yet rising sea levels and erosion of land is only part of the problem for this historic island: the land in and around the Chesapeake is actually sinking, for example, Hampton Roads is gradually sinking 5-7.5 inches per century, and though this may not seem like much to most, for the folks living in Tangier, only 36 inches above sea level, every inch matters.

The BBC recently stated that "fishing restrictions, erosion, and rising sea levels have resulted in most of the younger members of this tightly-knit community looking for opportunities elsewhere."

If you want to visit America's most fascinating island, you had better hurry… fortunately, ferry boats run to and from the island every day. Sign me up!

Michigan Woman Targeted Because She Shares Name With Unpopular Massachusetts Politician
Appalachian Magazine Staff

Hell hath no fury quite like a roving mob of angry keyboardists thousands of miles away: a reality one Michigan woman has been forced to face this week.

Michelle Dubois is a Michigan stay at home mother and does graphic design work on the side. She is a wife, homeschool mom, pet owner and by all accounts a likable person; unfortunately for her, 758 miles to the east, there is another Michelle Dubois, a 43-year-old Democrat serving in the Massachusetts House of Representatives and in March 2017, Rep. Dubois garnered national headlines when she tipped off the public that ICE was planning a raid in Brockton, Massachusetts.

Up to this point, Michigan's Michelle DuBois had never heard of Massachusetts' Michelle DuBois, but all of this was about to change.

"When the first messages came in I was left to put the puzzle together why people were sending me messages that I should go to jail," stated the Michigan homeschool mother in an interview with *Appalachian Magazine.*

Another message stated, "Wait til someone harms a member of your family who's here illegally and see how it affects your life FOREVER!"

From there, a steady stream of messages continued to flow into her Facebook account as commenters considered every portion of the Michigan woman's life to be fair game. Taking jabs that were way too personal.

Even DuBois' husband received a comment from a Greensboro, North Carolina, man calling the woman an "ugly witch" and even going so far as to allege that the couple's children weren't his... and that was some of the nicer parts of the individual's comment.

In an attempt to put an end to the hostile messages, she posted a comment with a link to the Massachusetts lawmaker's story stating, "This is not me. So the hate mail can stop.

We don't even live in the same state people."

Sadly, this didn't help in the slightest bit, as the post received more than 40 comments from people calling her "Anti-American" to more bizarre exchanges such as the one below:

  typical liberal piece of shit illegals first americans last why is it the ugliest women hate this country or is it because your so ugly its the only way you can get attention
Like · Reply · 14 hrs

> Michelle Dubois Are you calling me ugly or the State Representative who did that? Because I am not her. . .But you can see my profile picture.
>
> Like · Reply · 2 · 14 hrs

> Michelle Dubois no not you the state representive who did this saw your picture you cute and i hope a good american
> Like · Reply · 1 · 14 hrs

"But people didn't read what I wrote, they just yelled at me," she said.

Speaking of another commenter, DuBois stated, "I was called a 'c***' and that he hoped I was 'raped by an illegal alien' and even once the man realized he had the wrong person he still referred to me as a 'c***' to my husband."

In a last ditch effort, DuBois changed her profile picture, putting her graphic design skills to work (photo on bottom right of page was made her Facebook profile picture).

Unfortunately, she continued to get hate messages for another week until, fortunately for her, the story began dying down and the angry mob of Internet users grabbed their pitchforks and torches in search of their next victim.

The day prior to receiving the messages,

227

the mother, wife and graphic design artist could have never imagined what the coming week would bring.

"Thankfully, I have a pretty good sense of humor. I have been able to laugh at a number of the comments because people just don't understand. I know they aren't actually directed at me. Though some were overboard and I deleted them right away."

When you say your prayers this evening, remember a Michigan mother and beg God that you don't happen to share a name with the next national newsmaker.

Remembering the Tough Jobs of
Bowling Alley Pinboys
Appalachian Magazine Staff

Believe it or not, but the game of bowling is one of the oldest sports still being played today.

Dating back more than 3,000 years before Christ, the ancient Romans and Egyptians both played games we would immediately recognize as "bowling". Early bowling balls were made using the husks of grains, covered in leather and bound with string. Other balls made of porcelain have also been found, indicating that these were rolled along the ground rather than thrown due to their size and weight.

About 400 AD bowling began in Germany as a religious ritual to cleanse oneself from sin by rolling a rock into a club representing the heathen, over the next thousand years, the ceremony would evolve into sport and in 1325 laws were passed in Berlin and Cologne limiting bets on bowling to five shillings.

In 1366 the first official mention of bowling in England was made when King Edward III banned it as a distraction to archery practice.

Over the next several centuries, the game's popularity remained fairly stagnant until an influx of German immigrants introduced the age-old game to a new generation of Americans and in 1840, the first indoor bowling alley opened in New York City.

In September 1895 the modern standardized rules for ten-pin bowling were established in New York City and soon bowling alleys began popping up around the country.

In an era before the many mechanical advancements bowling alleys now enjoy, fallen pins had to be removed and stood back up entirely by hand and in the opening days of the 20th century, child labor provided just the workforce to do this.

With space between the pins and the back wall being limited, small boys, often no older than nine-years-old, would squeeze themselves into position in order to stand pins and lift the heavy bowling balls into the return chute.

In May 1907, Marion, Ohio's The Marion Mirror, documented the work of "pin boys":

"The regulation pin weights a little more than three pounds and the whole set weighs approximately 35 pounds... The largest number of balls a player can roll in a ten-inning game is 21, and the smallest eleven. Splitting the difference, a good blower may be said to average sixteen balls weighing 716 pounds... for a five-men team, the boy lifts balls weighing 3,580 pounds and adding the amount lifted in pins and balls, the much-abused pin setter lifts in one evening 9,174 pounds.... He lifts almost five tons in one night."

Sadly, the job of the pin boy was among the most thankless jobs in the nation in the early 1900s.

Working in the smoke-filled, alcohol flowing, profanity-laced underworld of yesteryear, pin boys were often blamed by bowlers for "interfering" with "wobbling pins" too soon, thus preventing strikes.

In no time, the industry came under the careful scrutiny of the United States Children's Bureau as youth could be found laboring in the smoky bar room atmosphere until midnight or later.

On January 18, 1914, The Washington Times, published an article entitled, "Pin Boy's Path is Not Flowerly One", in which they showcased the plight of the child-laborers:

"No matter how many pins fly up and caress him on the forehead, he must stick to his post. being able to withstand the attack of tall ten of the pins in his alley and half-dozen or so from that of his neighbors' is part of his business."

According to the report, pin boys were paid, "One dollar a day on the days that he works the curses and slanders of an indiscriminating bowling public, and a body full of black and blue bruises which can't always be seen, for most of our pin boys in Washington are of such a hue that the black and blue marks cannot always be discerned from the rest of the surface."

The 1930s brought considerable child labor crackdowns, the Great Depression and the invention of the mechanical pinsetter, all of which worked together to eliminate the jobs of pin boys.

So the next time you go bowling, take a moment and silently thank the hundreds of pin boys who endured bruises, cursings and deplorable working conditions in order to make bowling popular in America!

Kentucky & Virginia: North of New Jersey

Appalachian Magazine Staff

We all know that the Commonwealths of Virginia and Kentucky are both southern states.

Likewise, we are also fully aware of the reality that there's no question that New Jersey is a northern state. Right?

These truths have been well defined for centuries and there are few individuals who will ever question these statements as being factual.

But in the words of the great Lee Corso, "Not so fast, my friend!"

It seems the map may disagree with this assessment. Believe it or not, but there are portions of the Bluegrass State in which one can actually be standing north of beachgoers on the Jersey Shore.

Furthermore, Virginia, the capital of the Confederacy, actually has two counties that are entirely north of the Garden State's southern shoreline — in fact, Virginia's northernmost point in Frederick County, Virginia, is a full 37 miles north of New Jersey's southernmost point.

Who doesn't love a good ole fashioned geographic oddity?

Here are just a handful of other geographic oddities to wet your map studying whistle:

- Virginia's Lee County is actually west of Detroit, Michigan
- West Virginia stretches farther north than Brooklyn, New York
- A ship entering the Panama Canal from the Atlantic Ocean will exit the canal in the Pacific Ocean east of where they first entered the canal (in the Atlantic).

DEAR READER,

We never could have imagined the exciting opportunities that awaited us the morning we clicked the "publish" button on our Appalachian blog for the first time. The stories we shared were tales of the only people and places our grandparents ever knew and they were incredible.

It saddens me that my grandparents never lived to see the day the stories of them ringing the outside dinner bell to warn their cousins that the revenuers were in town or that pictures of the family's century old cemetery would be viewed by millions of people around the globe.

They were proud of the place they called home and so am we.

As the publication has taken wings of its own, we fully recognize the incredible responsibility that has been thrust upon us — a responsibility to use our reach for the betterment of the thousands of map dots from Georgia to Pennsylvania.

With this understanding in mind, great pains have been taken to ensure this print-publication has highlighted the people, customs and places of home in an honest and honorable manner.

It is our sincerest prayer, that *Appalachian Magazine's Mountain Voice: 2017* is only the first of many great editions to come.

We look forward to getting to know you better in the days ahead!

Thank you,

Jeremy + Allison Farley

CONTACT US

To invite Jeremy Farley to a speaking engagement, please contact via the email listed below:

We'd love to hear from you, keep in touch:

<u>Facebook:</u>
Facebook.com/AppalachianMagazine

<u>Twitter:</u>
@AppalachianMag

<u>Email:</u>
publisher@appalachianmagazine.com

<u>Website:</u>
www.AppalachianMagazine.com